London Dockland

Professor S K Al Naib

Luxury trades, like jewellery, depended upon overseas markets.

Work at St Katharine's, 1827, reflects the enormous engineering achievements of the early docks.

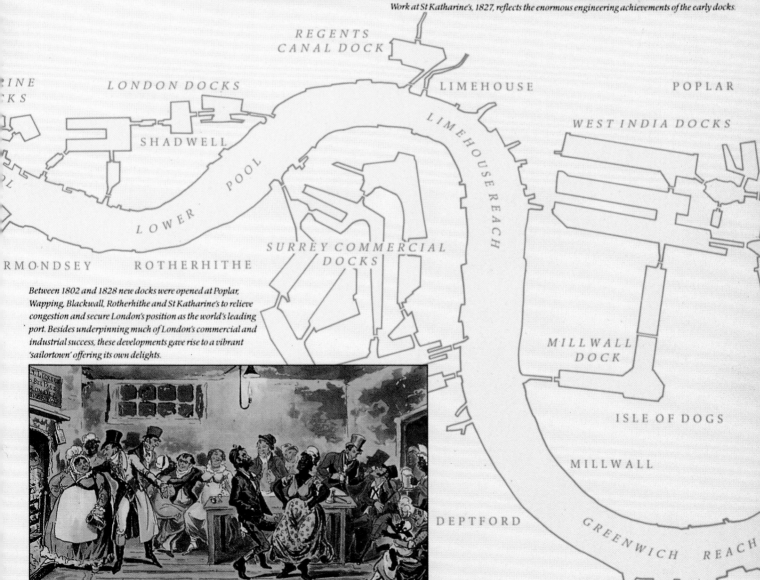

REGENTS CANAL DOCK

LONDON DOCKS

LIMEHOUSE

POPLAR

SHADWELL

WEST INDIA DOCKS

LIMEHOUSE REACH

LOWER POOL

SURREY COMMERCIAL DOCKS

RMONDSEY

ROTHERHITHE

MILLWALL DOCK

ISLE OF DOGS

MILLWALL

DEPTFORD

GREENWICH REACH

GREE

Between 1802 and 1828 new docks were opened at Poplar, Wapping, Blackwall, Rotherhithe and St Katharine's to relieve congestion and secure London's position as the world's leading port. Besides underpinning much of London's commercial and industrial success, these developments gave rise to a vibrant 'sailortown' offering its own delights.

The Illustrated Guide for Londoners and Visitors

Londoners may remember little about their historic port, of the infinite variety and immense quantities of goods which passed in and out each day, and may not realise that it was owing to this trade that the City of London in the main owed its position as the financial centre of the World. Goods from many countries constantly entered and left the city.

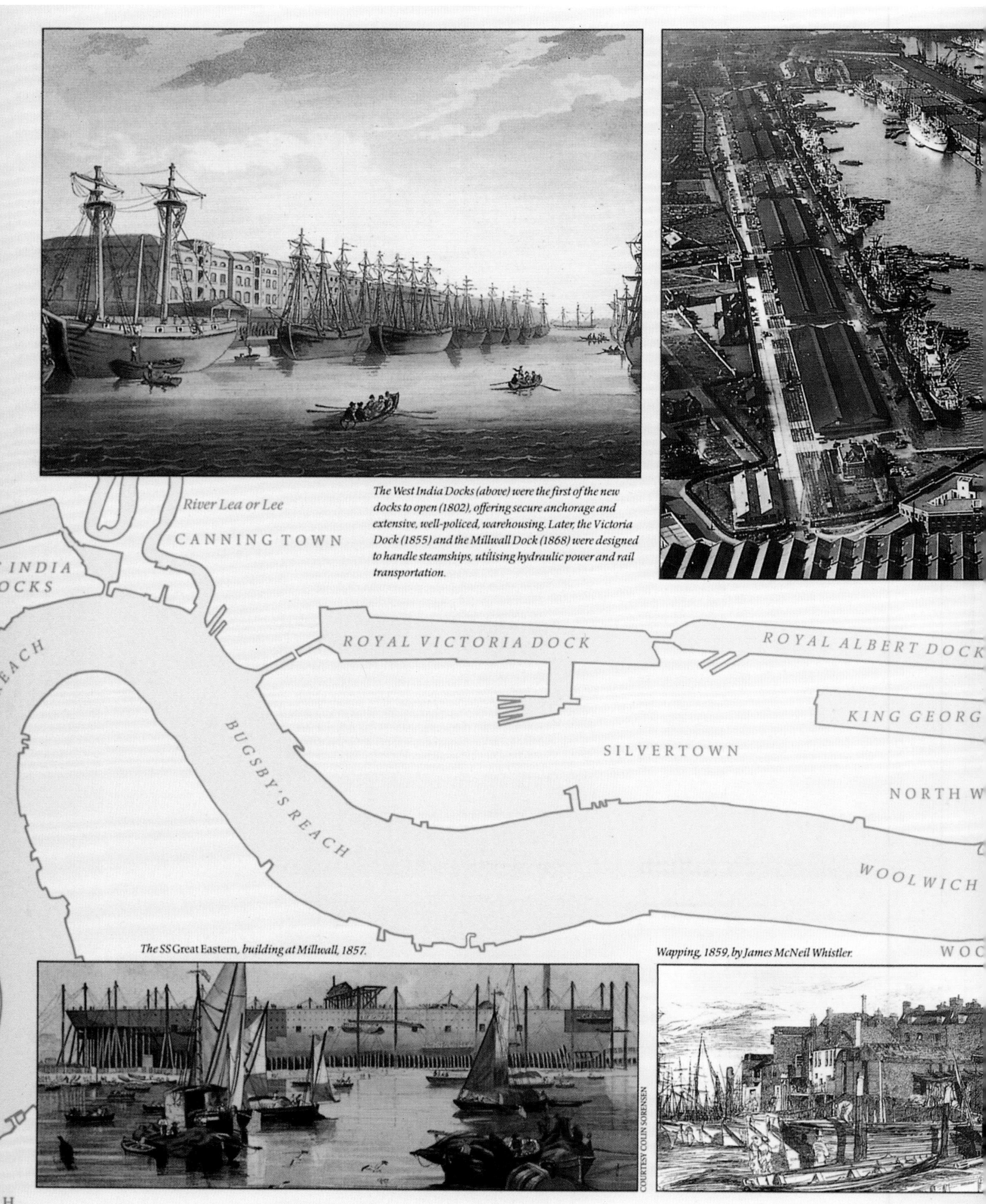

The West India Docks (above) were the first of the new docks to open (1802), offering secure anchorage and extensive, well-policed, warehousing. Later, the Victoria Dock (1855) and the Millwall Dock (1868) were designed to handle steamships, utilising hydraulic power and rail transportation.

The SS Great Eastern, building at Millwall, 1857.

Wapping, 1859, by James McNeil Whistler.

This book tells the colourful story of London Docklands and its people from Roman times through its heydays of the 19th and 20th centuries to the present day. It traces the steps by which London as a port, acquired its position of pre-eminence and shows how in recent years is providing a model for the rest of the World in its regeneration programme to secure the future of the capital as the leading city into the 21st century. Enjoy discovering Docklands.

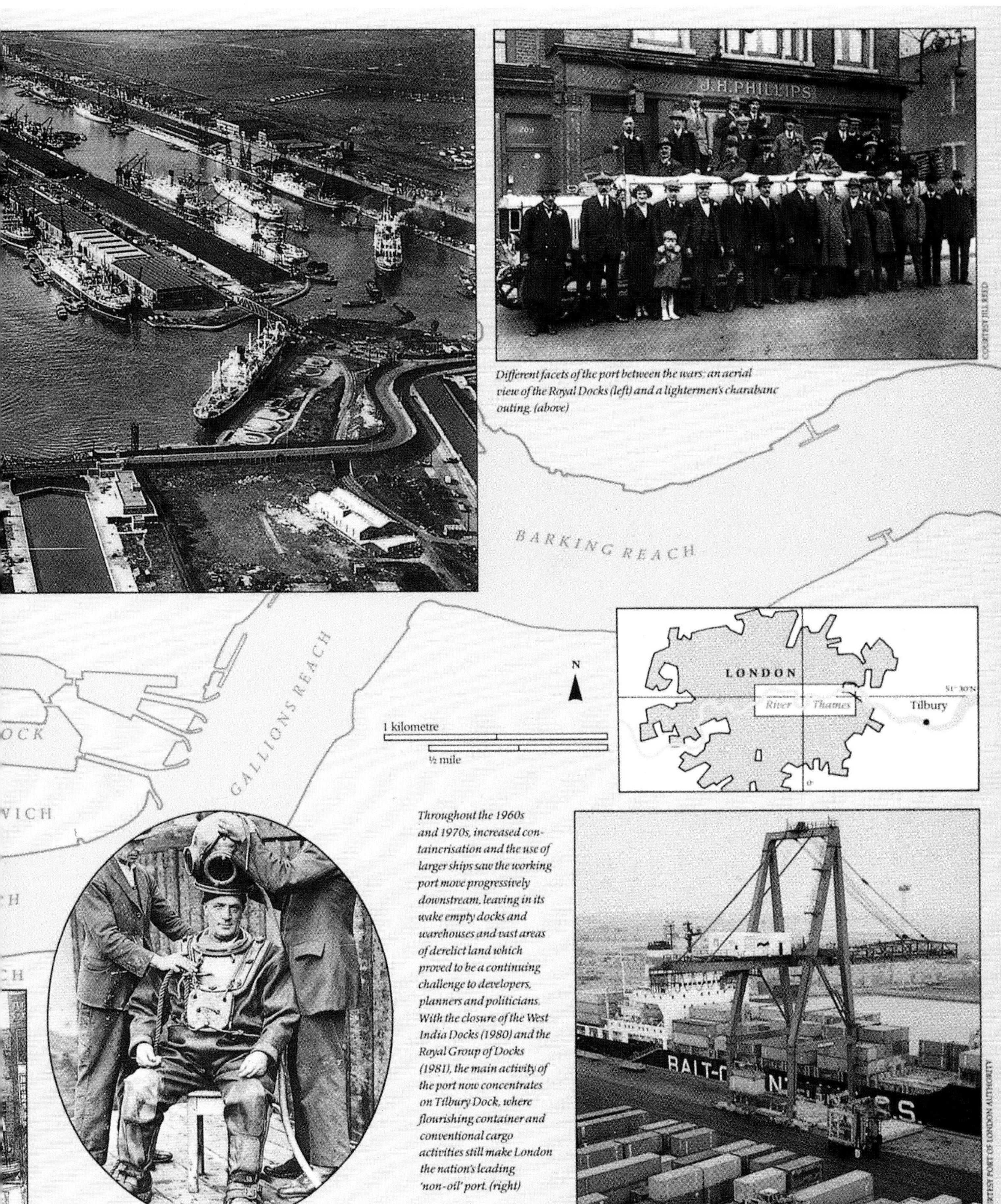

Different facets of the port between the wars: an aerial view of the Royal Docks (left) and a lightermen's charabanc outing. (above)

Throughout the 1960s and 1970s, increased containerisation and the use of larger ships saw the working port move progressively downstream, leaving in its wake empty docks and warehouses and vast areas of derelict land which proved to be a continuing challenge to developers, planners and politicians. With the closure of the West India Docks (1980) and the Royal Group of Docks (1981), the main activity of the port now concentrates on Tilbury Dock, where flourishing container and conventional cargo activities still make London the nation's leading 'non-oil' port. (right)

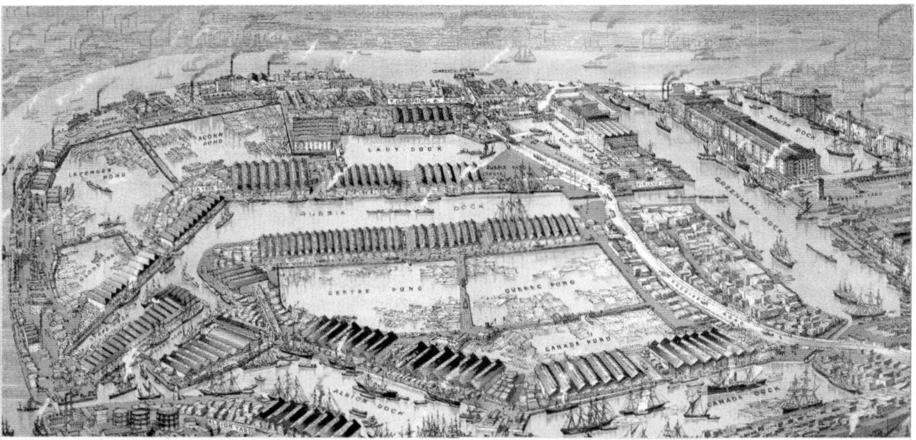

a) A bird's eye view of Surrey Commercial Docks looking east, c 1906. (b) Brunel's Thames Tunnel from Wapping to Rotherhithe, opened 1843, (c) Britain's tallest building, Canary Wharf on the Isle of Dogs, 1994. (d) Panorama of today's Docklands.

Contents

Books by the Author

"London Dockland Guide" Visitors Pictorial Panorama **ISBN 18745 360 31**
"London illustrated" Historical, Current and Future. **ISBN 18745 360 15**
"Discover London Docklands" A to Z Illustrated Guide. **ISBN 18745 360 07**
"Hydraulic Structures" Theory, Analysis and Design. **ISBN 0901 987 83 2**
"London Docklands" Past, Present and Future. **ISBN 1874 5360 23**
"European Docklands" Past, Present and Future. **ISBN 0901 987 82 4**
"Dockland" Historical Survey **ISBN 0908 987 80 0**
"Applied Hydraulics" Theory and Solution Manual. **ISBN 1874 5360 58**

Order through: Research Books, P O Box 82, Romford, Essex, RM6 5BY, United Kingdom.

PREFACE

Welcome to London Docklands - a huge area on the River Thames on the east side of London. At first glance this whole area appears to be a complex of tall concrete buildings a little like the giant cranes that used to be so busy loading and unloading cargo from the ships that used to come here. But the buildings and cranes are linked not only to the Docklands past but to Docklands future. The Docklands of today is a mix of historic renovations and modern architecture, office buildings, leisure facilities, shopping centres and every type of luxury living available and the thread which links all these together is water. Everywhere you look there is a spectacular river view.

In its heyday, Docklands was a lively and bustling sort of place with goods coming from all parts of the world - there was jute from India, bananas from the Caribbean and tobacco from Virginia. Thousands of the legendary dockers were employed in this area; in fact the whole area developed a unique character all its own. As you look at the historical evidence it is hard to imagine that these docks are now empty. Only their names recall the past. The big containers finally took the ships away to deeper waters at Tilbury and the waterside warehouses were left to decay. Today, romantic sounding names such as Gun Wharves, Butlers Wharves and Dickens Inn are bursting with new life. For this is London Docklands and its story is a modern Cinderella. Please come with me on a journey of discovery through East London over the past two hundred years....

ISBN 1874 5 360 31

First Printing August 1996

The author is Professor of Civil Engineering and Head of Department at the University of East London, England. (Tel: 0181 590 7722/7000 ext 2478/2531)

Printed by The KPC Group, London and Ashford, Kent.

Early History of Britain's Greatest Port

The Port Beginnings

London Docklands lies within the flood plain of the lower Thames and its tributaries. The area consisted of riverside marshland before the massive engineering projects of the 19th century took place. From its scenic source in the hills of Gloucestershire, the River winds its way gracefully to the sea. It is one of the world's most famous rivers for its history, its beauty and its vital role in the shaping of Britain's destiny over the past two centuries. Along its last 69 miles, from the tidal waters at Teddington to the Estuary, the river was once the major artery of the Nation and the World.

The port was founded two thousand years ago when a settlement was established at a point near London Bridge where it was possible at low tide to cross the Thames. Here a gravel stratum on Corn Hill on the north bank faced a gravel bed projecting from the Southwark marshes and a deep pool formed where ships could lie. In AD43, the Roman legions under their Emperor Claudius invaded Britain and made Londinium as its capital. Subsequently, the port developed along the City of London waterfront until the Middle Ages when the riverside wharves started to spread into the marshlands outside the city walls. Some of today's dockland areas such as Shadwell, Bermondsey and Rotherhithe were inhabited.

London's seaborne merchandise was mainly loaded to and from ships moored in the Pool of London or, when the latter become congested, in the river downstream and then carried by barges or wherries to the hithes, quays and warehouses of the City. Of the other hithes, Billingsgate overlooked the Pool and accommodated sea vessels at its wharves. It was here that the King's custom officers principally assessed and levied tolls on the cargoes. The great English poet, Geoffrey Chaucer, who was born in Thames Street, was appointed in 1374 as Controller of the Customs of Wool, Skins and Tanned Hides in the City. The first Customs House was established at Woolwich in 1382 under his direction.

The City Legal Quays

The Tudor period saw an increase in the spirit of enterprise amongst the merchants and ship owners of London which advanced the nation's prestige and foreign trade. In 1515 King Henry VIII set up the Royal Dockyards at Deptford and Woolwich. Sir Hugh Willoughby and Richard Chancellor sailed from Deptford in 1553 which resulted in opening up trade with Russia. Huge developments took place in Elizabethan times and London collected half

The Changing Face of London *Left:(a) Conjectural view of Londinium from the south east during the reign of Hadrian, circa AD125. (b) Rhinebeck water-colour of the city, River and Custom House, circa 1810.(c) The City of London today with old Billingsgate Fish Market, Custom House Quay and Tower Pier along the Thames. Right: A series of aerials showing today's London Docklands including Surrey Quays, Isle of Dogs, Wapping, Rotherhithe, St Katherine Docks, London City Airport and Greenland Docks.*

the Customs revenue in the country. In order to ensure for the Crown its due share in Customs duties Queen Elizabeth I appointed a Royal Commission in 1558 to select twenty `Legal Quays' at which all dutiable goods were to be landed. All these were sited between London Bridge and the Tower. In course of time these facilities became inadequate and 'Sufferance Wharves' were established in Bermondsey on the south bank with restricted privileges.

The port grew through the centuries and ship building, timber, cooperage, armaments and vitalling all flourished in the riverside areas. The volume of river traffic became too much for the legal quays and sufferance wharves to handle and vessels had to lay at anchor waiting to be unloaded. By 1783 cargo from ships had reached incredible proportions and action was required to relieve the congestion.

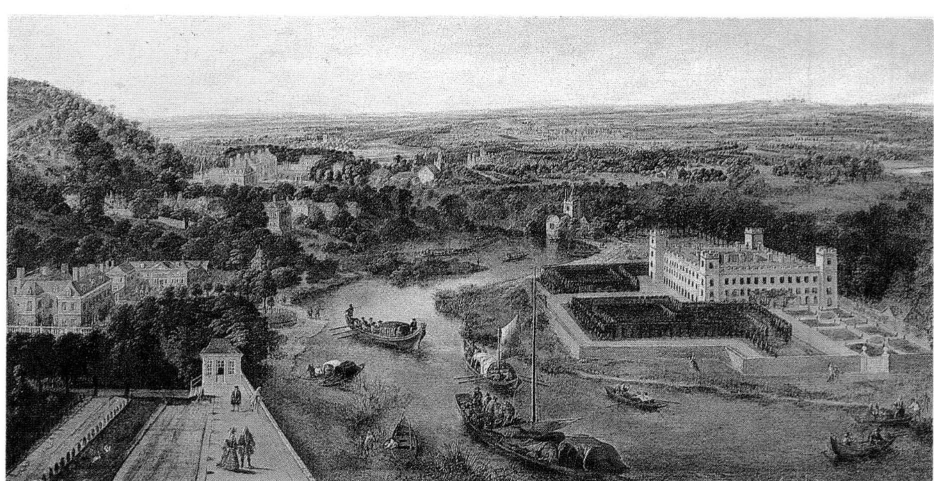

Old Scenic Views along the River Thames
(a) Canaletto's painting of Royal College at Greenwich with its peaceful river activities.
(b) Syon House at Brentford where the Romans probably crossed the river when they first arrived. Painting by Jan Griffier, circa 1668.
(c) A vibrant wedding by the River Thames in Bermondsey during the reign of Queen Elizabeth I, on the spot where Butlers Wharf and the Circle Development are today. Note the Monks from the nearby Bermondsey Monastery seen on the right.

Great Britain In The World Of 1783

Until the 16th century Britain remained on the fringe of the old world which centred around the Mediterranean Sea. The discovery of the New World revolutionised the importance of European countries on the Atlantic seaboard and they began to benefit the trading advantages of their positions. Britain was most active in this respect and developed a superiority in commerce, trade and industry and the advantages enjoyed by the British Isles were many. Their insular character gave security, the indented coast provided excellent harbours and brought all parts of the interior within easy access of the shores. The mineral wealth of coal and iron provided the raw materials necessary for the development of manufacturing and the start of the industrial revolution. Britain's colonial possessions were a valuable source of raw materials and food. The predominant position of British shipping in the commerce of the world and the power of the Navy to protect, gave Britain the means of carrying her imports and exports safely all over the world.

The foundations of a new British Empire were already laid in 1783 when William Pitt became Prime Minister. The loss of the American Colonies was a big blow, but Canada remained loyal and Britain retained an important foothold on the North American Continent. The defeat of the French in India had made Britain predominant and her gradual penetration of the sub-continent was not hampered. Captain Cook's scientific expeditions to Australia (1769-1774) had opened up a new field of activity for British enterprise and migration in Australia and New Zealand. A few coastal settlements in Africa were important because of the slave trade and their positions enroute to India and the Far East. Islands in the West Indies were the most cherished of all British possessions in the days when Britain was self-sufficient as regards wheat and meat, for the sugar, cotton, rum, fruit juice, tobacco and mahogany brought from them were the staple commodities of overseas trade and the wealth of the City of London.

This rapid expansion caused serious problems of congestion in the port in the second half of the 18th century. Although there was room at the mooring piers for 600 ships there were occasions when seasonal traders, such as those carrying sugar form the West Indies, swelled that number to as many as 1400. The inadequacy of the existing quays in handling the growing quantities of merchandise meant that ships often moored in the river for months blocking the passage of other vessels and providing a source of plunder for pilfers and river pirates. According to the man whose idea led to the formation of the Thames Police Force a license to plunder could be obtained for 20-30 guineas a night (around £25). It became evident that unless wharfage for ships increased, the future development of London as a trading centre of the world would suffer.

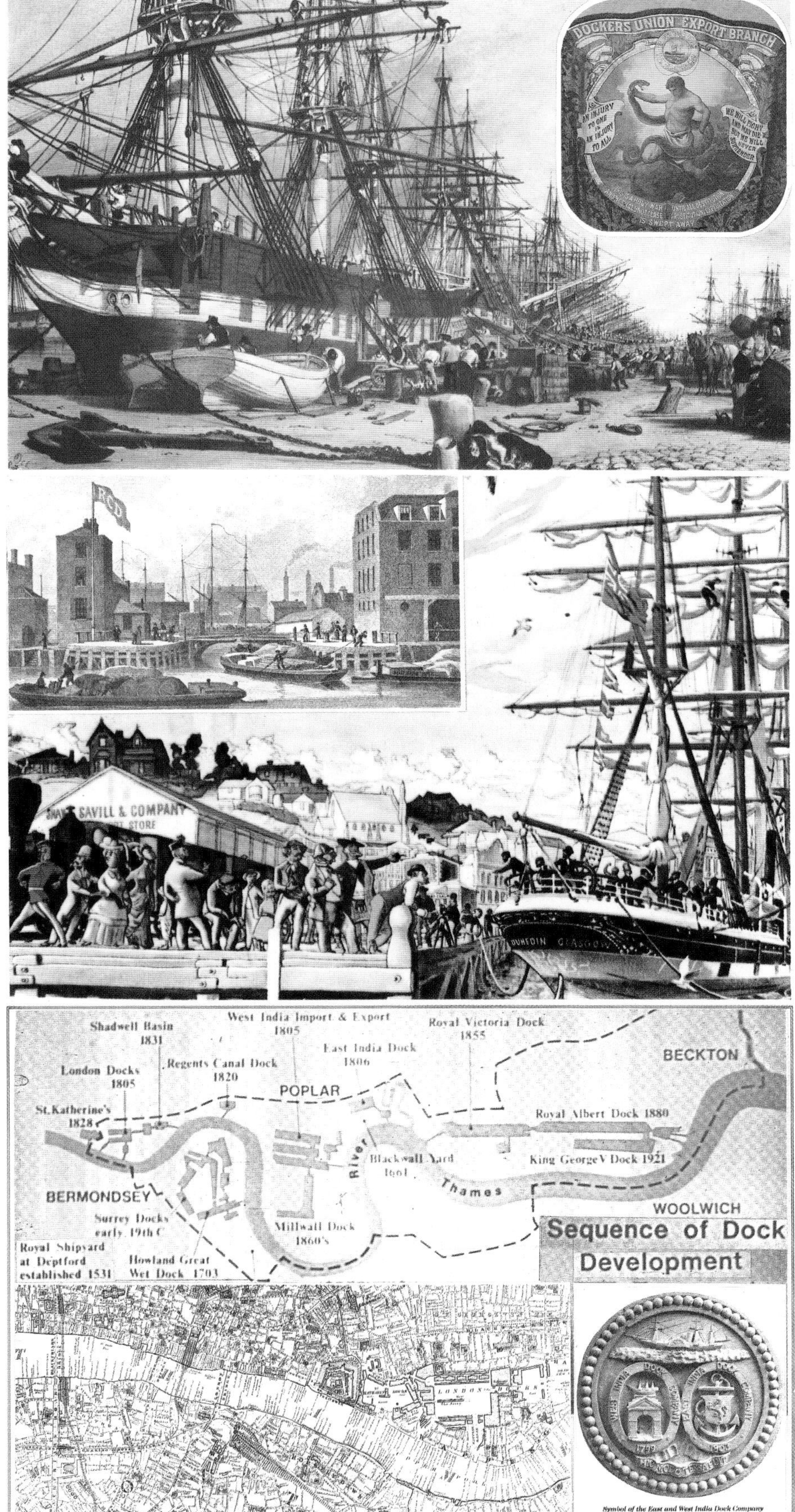

(a) Busy quayside scene at the West India Import Dock c1830. On board the ships the crews carry out routine maintenance to masts and rigging. (b) The "Dunedin" carrying the first historic cargo of frozen meat from New Zealand bound for London c1882. The inset is the river entrance to Regent Canal Dock, Limehouse 1828. (c) The sequence of dock development in London including a map of 1862.

London Georgian Docks

In 1793 William Vaughan, a Director of Royal Exchange Assurance and a spokesman for the West India merchants, published the first proposals for a system of wet docks in London. The Corporation of London , which controlled the Legal Quays, resisted any plans for the wet docks, fearing a loss of revenue and power. So did the absentee landlords who owned the quays and were concerned about loss of rent. The guilds of porters also saw their livelihood threatened. However, the powerful merchants trading with the West Indies were the first to overcome these problems and defeat the vested interest. They won their Act to build the first dock on the Isle of Dogs which sparked the building boom of wet docks in east London. After a period of debate, the plan for building the West India docks was passed by Parliament in 1799, and for the building of the London docks in June 1800.

West India Docks 1800-1806

The West India Docks were built on reclaimed marshland and on the eve of completion William Daniell published his famous engraving. The speed and care with which the building was undertaken was remarkable. The excavated material was used to raise the surrounding land by 6-12 ft above high water level. It was also turned into bricks for the works, although extra bricks were brought downriver from Brentford. The bottoms of the docks were lined in puddled clay, 12" thick with entrances at each end. The Blackwall Entrance Lock which survives today, was completed in 1802. It was the largest of its kind and beautifully constructed with counter bolts and masonry facings. The first north quay warehouses were designed by George Gwilt and his son. The warehouses were the grandest and most commodious ever seen. The developers of present day Canary Wharf had in mind the most important objectives of the design guidelines was to generate such an awareness after a period of 185 years.

In the course of construction there were a couple of disasters due to collapse but it was altogether an extraordinary achievement in such a short time. Costing £1.2million and immediately earning £200,000 p.a., it was an instant success. This was due to the privilege which ensured that all of the West Indies trade had to be handled at the dock for the first twenty-one years, an arrangement which can be likened to the setting up of the Enterprise Zone n today's Docklands. The foundation stone promised an undertaking which would contribute stability, increase and ornament to British commerce.

London Docks 1801-1805

Meanwhile, in July 1800, Daniel Alexander was appointed as Surveyor and Architect for the London Dock at Wapping. John Rennie was appointed engineer in May 1801, with James Murray as resident engineer from September. Steam engines were used in the construction of this dock for drainage, mixing mortar and pile driving, the latter being the first recorded example of steam pile driving. Also for the first time a stationary steam engine was used to haul wagons up an inclined plane to remove spoil from the excavation. The London Dock was opened on 31st January 1805 and showed Rennie at the height of his powers. The total cost to 1806 was about £2.1million of which more than half was due to the purchase of property. Having a smaller burden of capital outlay to carry, the West India scheme was a financial success from the outset.

East India Docks 1803-1806

Shortly afterwards the East India Company came up with proposals for docks of their own at Blackwall. In 1782 the company had erected commodious and imposing warehouses in the City of London at Cutler Street. Imports such as silks and spices were of high value in relation to their weight and bulk, and could be easily transported from Blackwall - the furthest point up river to which the large East Indiamen ships could conveniently approach and where they lay at anchor - to the City by horse drawn van for warehousing

(a) An elevated view of the West India Docks and Warehouses on the Isle of Dogs on the eve of completion 1802. The engraving by William Daniell shows the river frontage along Coldharbour and the Blackwall Basin.(b) An engraving of the East India Docks looking south, the Isle of Dogs on the right and River Lea on the left of the picture. (c) An engraving of the magnificent warehouses on the North Quay of West India Import Dock.

Top: (a) Opening of St Katharine Docks,October 1828. (b) St Katharine Docks in 1829, showing the clock tower and Telford's bridge. (c) Busy scene in the Pool of London. Middle: (d) The North Quay of London Docks showing activities of a discharging vessel. The dockers are handling wine and wool products, c1823. (e) The Wapping Dock entrance and a forest of sailing ship masts, 1820s. Bottom: (f) Bird's eye view of London Docks and the river, c1845. (g) London, Pleasure Boats - For a 150 years the "Butterfly Boats" of the River Thames paddled their way up and down the river and out to Southend, Margate, Ramsgate and Dover, where trippers spent a day at the seaside. The engraving shows a view from London Bridge looking down river to the Tower, c1844. The Custom House and London Bridge Wharf are on the left where passengers can be seen embarking for Gravesend and Margate.

The East India Company obtained an Act for its docks in July 1803 and appointed John Rennie and Ralph Walker to be their engineers in August. The old Brunswick Dock was transformed into a new Export Dock and further inland a larger dock basin was constructed which was to serve as the Company's Import Dock. The entrance lock, similar to those of the West India and London Docks, was 210 feet long, 48 feet wide, and 25 feet deep, and could accommodate the largest East Indiaman of the time (1500 tons) though not fully laden. Even after the East India Docks were opened the Company's largest ships had to partially unload down-river in Long Reach before proceeding to the docks at Blackwall. Nevertheless the East India dock entrance was the largest in the world till 1838 and was not exceeded in London until the Victoria Dock was opened in 1855.

Surrey Docks 1800-1811

On the South bank meanwhile, the Surrey Dock system was beginning to take shape. The Grand Surrey Canal, an ambitious scheme proposed in 1800, was intended to run from Rotherhithe to Epsom via Croydon and be lined with market gardens whose would be transported to London, but the waterway only reached Camberwell with a branch to Peckham. In the following years other docks and basins were opened. The old Greenland Dock of 1700 was improved in 1810 and Rotherhithe became a thriving waterfront for shipping.

East End Fortress

Except on the Surrey side, the docks were built like fortresses with high walls surrounding them and the few gates were manned by private police forces. Those guarding the West India Docks were organised on para-military lines, armed with pistols and cutlasses and protected by a moat. A considerable length of the original 6m high boundary wall of the East India Docks constructed in 1806 still remains intact. These were designed to secure the East India Company's cargo from pilferage.

Also in the area of the East India Docks the company had its own prison. Blackwall Yard situated between the disused Brunswick Wharf power station and Charrington Road terminal was laid out in 1587 to repair ships and was later used by the East India Dock Company for handling cargoes discharged from ships moored in the River Thames. The yard also built ships and between 1612 and 1901 launched more than 550 East Indiamen battle ships, frigates, tea clippers and mail steamers. Two graving docks, in use until the early 1980s, were still visible in 1996.

The building of the first great docks in the Port of London created the biggest construction site in the World and could be considered the birth and establishment of the profession of civil engineering in the public eye. The three docks were in full working order by 1806 having been built on a scale without precedent in this or any other country and within the amazingly short time of six years.

During this period a number of civil engineering methods were developed which could be considered as firsts and these newly developed techniques were used in the construction of the St Katharine docks.

St Katharines Docks 1827-1828

The amount of dock building which took place in London during the first two decades of the nineteenth century makes this period almost one of dock mania. Indeed we have not quite finished with the building of what might be termed London's Georgian docks. Of these older docks one group remains to be discussed. St. Katharine Docks built 1827-8, on the north bank by the Tower, is perhaps best known of all the docks as the basins and central warehouse, "I" Warehouses of 1858, have survived and are open to the general public as a leisure amenity. The scheme for the St. Katharine Docks was something of an unnecessary speculation; London already had sufficient dock accommodation but the site, close to the City, attracted investors, prompted by the impending expiry of the 21 year monopolies granted to the first dock companies. The space needed to build the docks was already occupied by densely packed housing for the poor, a brewery, and a medieval religious foundation, the Royal Katharine, which, because of Royal patronage, had escaped the full rigors of the reformation in the 16th century. It is from this religious foundation that the docks take their name. Thomas Telford, nearing the end of his distinguished career, was appointed engineer with the young Philip Hardwick as architect. By January 1828 an engraving showed the walls of the basins well advanced. It was said that during construction a thousand men were employed in the excavations. However, more than 1100 houses were demolished and the tenants evicted without any compensation.

The opening of St Katharines Docks on 25th October 1828 firmly established the profession of civil engineering. The small society of Civil Engineers which formed in 1818 became the Institution of Civil Engineers and was Chartered and honoured with Thomas Telford as its first President.

Left: (a) London Dock entrance at Wapping, c1830s, showing the lock machinery and a steamship entering a busy dock, early 19th century. Note the horse-drawn cart laden with wool. (b) The opening of St Katherine Docks, October 1828, showing the arrival of the first vessel laden with sugar. The Bell House is shown on the left. Note the welcoming crowd of merchants and shipping officials. (c) Surrey Commercial riverside scene at Rotherhithe, early 19th century, showing vessels discharing forest products. Note the heavy timber crane on the right with the nearby ferry boat. Right: (d) Bird's eye view of London Docks looking east, September 1845 (e) East India Docks and Mast House, July 1848 (f) Dredging the river bed in the Pool of London circa 1850.

The Great Warehouses

In the economy of a port, adequate provision for the safe keeping of cargo is almost as important as harbourage and ship discharge facilities. The Port of London established its principal cargo safe-deposit at the London and St Katherine Docks and at the Town Warehouses in Cutler Street. The warehouses became bonded, attended to by Customs Officers, for the import of a variety of goods including rice, wine, brandy and wool. Underground vaults stored wines and spirits.

The tobacco warehouses were also one of the great curiosities of the time. The vast quantities brought into the Port of London were stored prior to being entered for consumption or export. The warehouses occupied some 5 acres of the eastern extremity of the London Docks. There were two warehouses, the smaller one being situated on the other side of the bridge which crossed the entrance to the docks from the river. On first entering the building of the larger warehouse glancing down the aisle stretching an immense distance, one could see hedged on either side huge casks resembling the sugar casks that could be seen at the doors of grocers. These casks were intermixed with large wooden square shaped packages filled with the closely pressed leaves of the tobacco plant. Here and there in this wilderness of casks would be seen a busy group assembled around a huge pair of scales, which required the assistance of a huge pulley wheel fixed to the beams of the roof above to hoist them free of the ground. A number of workmen would be busily employed opening the casks. When the head had been removed together with the upper hoops, the cask was tilted by the combined efforts of three or four pairs of arms upon one board of the scale and taken off like a big bale leaving the contents standing in a solid column of tightly pressed tobacco leaves.

Thomas Telford

A London sailing barge.

Top: (a) East India Dock showing dockers landing Indian tea chests from a clipper for storage in the quay warehouse. Note the two and four-wheeled hand trucks. (b) The Wool Warehouse in the London Docks showing the well-lit floors. The lower ground shows the weight operation being performed on a beam scale, c1860. Bottom: (c) Breaking Bulk on board a tea ship in the London Docks, December 1877. The Chinese ship gangs loading onto platform boards for delivery to the quay. (d) The wine vaults in the London Docks guarded by the dock policeman. Note the gas lighting and hand held oil lamp. (e) Inside the Tobacco Dock Warehouse showing the varied operations such as stacking, weighing and sampling for HM Customs and merchants.

London Victorian Docks

Ship Building (1835 - 1855)

The success and concentration of the Georgian docks in London attracted engineers from the north to establish sites along the river for ship building. In 1835 William Fairbairn acquired a site at Millwall where more than 100 vessels were built during the next thirteen years. It was reputed to be the first major ship building yard in Britain.

The most famous ship built on the Thames was the Great Eastern designed and constructed by the engineer Isambard Kingdom Brunel. The vessel was built in the yards of Millwall Ironworks and its sheer size made it a great engineering achievement of the 19th century. Over two thousand men and boys were employed in its construction but when it was finally launched it was found to be too costly to operate and too cumbersome for long voyages in rough seas. After first being used as a cable laying ship, then a passenger ship, it was laid up in Milford Haven in 1874. The Great Eastern was last used as a travelling exhibition and fun fair and in 1891 taken to Birkenhead to be broken up.

In 1984 where the former site of Burrells Wharf was being prepared for a new housing estate, the contractors uncovered what turned out to be one of the two slipways from which the Great Eastern had been launched, with great timbers laid out in piles and cross pieces sloping down to the waters edge. This discovery has been preserved as a memorial to the ship and the men who built it.

The Royal Victoria Dock 1855

By the 1850s steam had established itself at sea as the means of propulsion and large iron ships were rapidly replacing wooden ones. The docks constructed up to this time were for sailing ships whose size was limited by their timber construction and in fact seldom reached 1,500 tons. An Act of Parliament was obtained for making a new dock, one and a quarter miles long on the north bank, using the East Ham marshes downstream of Bow Creek. The promoters of the new "Victoria Dock", were not City men, nor did they have connections with the sea, they were men of the railway age, therefore direct communication with the national railway network was planned from the outset and the newly invented hydraulic power systems were installed. The Victoria Dock and the Graving Dock, (also known as the Pontoon Dock) were opened for business on the 26th November 1855 by Prince Albert and became an immediate financial success.

In December 1855 the gross registered tonnage of the vessels entering the dock was 31,500. Cargoes were silk, sugars, seed, corn, sulphur, timber etc. The docks were planned to occupy 90 acres of Plaistow marshes on the north bank of the Thames and adjoining the North Woolwich Railway by which they had ready access to the heart of the City and were placed in direct communication with the railways in the United Kingdom. All the cranes, capstans, lock gates and sluices were worked for the first time by hydraulic power. Messages were transmitted by electric telegraph from the dock house free of charge.

Trinity Buoy Wharf 1860

Nearby, the only lighthouse in London was constructed at Trinity Buoy Wharf in 1860 and used for a century as a centre for training of lighthouse keepers in the maintenance of lanterns. It provided a link between the old Corporation of Trinity House and Michael Faraday, the inventor and founding father of modern electricity.

Amalgamation of Dock Companies

The original dock companies did not continue unaltered throughout the nineteenth century and a considerable amount of take over and amalgamation took place. In 1838 the East and West India Dock companies combined against the competition of the St. Katharine and the London Docks. The East India Docks had no warehouses as the East India Company stored its goods at Cutler Street in the City and at that time there was surplus storage accommodation in the nearby West India docks providing inducement for amalgamation. The St. Katharine and the London docks had shallow river access, small entrance locks and no railway connections but plenty of warehouse accommodation. In contrast the Victoria dock, had opposite characteristics and there were clear advantages in the three companies combining, in 1864, to meet the competition of the amalgamated East and West India Docks. An amalgamation of this sort was made practical by the growing lighterage industry of the river - goods could be ferried up river in lighters from Victoria Docks to the older docks for warehousing.

Millwall Docks 1868

A decade after the opening of the Victoria Dock a new company appeared on the scene, the Millwall Dock Company, which constructed docks on the Isle of Dogs in 1868 to the south of the West India Docks. The Docks were not financially successful and in order to attract trade rates had to be kept very low. The Victorian period up to this time had done little to improve the life of the people.

The Millwall Outer Dock had the dry dock which was also known as the Millwall Graving Dock, because in the days of sail, graving consisted of scraping or burning off ships' hulls and then coating with tar. At first the ships which came in for repair or maintenance were mainly sailing ships and included such famous clippers as *Thermopylae* and her sister vessel the *Cutty Sark* which can be seen today at Greenwich. The dock is now a housing estate known as Clippers Quay.

Royal Albert Dock 1880

Owing to economic difficulties the intended extension of the Victoria Dock scheme eastwards did not take place until late 19th century. The new Royal Albert Dock was the first in London to be lit by electricity and was opened in 1880 by the Duke of Connaught. At the same time the prefix "Royal'" was added to the name of Victoria Dock.

Meat from New Zealand 1882

It was on 15th February 1882 that the first historic cargo of frozen produce left New Zealand's shore for Britain. That day the full rigged sailing ship "Dunedin", sailed from the south island's Port Chalmers bound for London. The ship was carrying 4311 carcasses of mutton, 598 carcasses of lamb, 22 pig carcasses, 2225 sheep tongues and several cartons of butter. The voyage was an experimental one to establish whether the cargo would last the long journey. Prior to this voyage New Zealand's agricultural exports to Britain had been limited to salted butter and cheese, some tinned meat and wool.

On 24th May 1882, some 98 days later, the *"Dunedin"* berthed at the East India Dock after a voyage of 12,000 miles. The cargo proved to be in excellent condition which was welcome news for London, hungry for food in the wake of the industrial revolution. (See page 7).

Tilbury Docks 1886

To meet the competition of the Royal Albert Dock, in 1886 the East and West India Dock Company opened new docks at Tilbury, 26 miles downstream from London Bridge. No warehouses were built at the docks but facilities were provided at a goods depot in Commercial Road, use being made of the London Tilbury and Southend Railway. The opening of Tilbury Docks proved to be one of the most significant developments in the history of the Port of London, with 75 acres of deep water berths and many large entrances. However in commercial terms the docks failed initially and the only way the docks could keep going was to cut their rates drastically. One shipping line was finally attracted after being offered a 50% reduction in rates for a whole ten-year period. Today, Tilbury Port is the only survivor of the Port of London and it is one of the most successful ports in the UK.

Building Labour and Dockers

The dock building labour force was brought in from other parts of the UK. The men were the counterparts of the labourers who had dug the canal system across the country and who later built roads and railways. Once the docks were completed, the labourers then became dockers. On 25th June 1872, the West India and Millwall Docks saw the first Dockers' strike, when they sought an increase from 4d to 6d (2½p) a day. The settlement was for 5d a day. Lt. Col. J Birt, the General Manager of the Millwall Docks, described the

The Royal Victoria, Albert and King George V Docks. Top: (a) The Royal Victoria during construction on Plaistow Marshes, September 1854 (b) Hydraulic lifts were used to float vessels in shallow waters for repairs, Victoria Graving Dock 1859. Middle: (c) Opening of the Royal Albert Dock by the Duke of Connaught and the Princess Royal aboard a paddle steamer, July 1880 (d) The Royal Yacht at the opening of King George V Dock 1921. In the background is Gallions Hotel which can be seen today. Bottom: (e) The Royal Victoria Dock and the western entrance, February 1856. A paddle steamer can be seen in the lock. (f) Unloading the Arowa on the north quay of the Royal Albert Dock, 1870. Note the cask work on the quay and rail operation.

casual dock workers to Parliament as "the poor fellows who are miserably clad, scarcely a boot on their feet".

It was said that the unemployed Londoners streamed down to the Isle of Dogs and worked as casual labourers. In some cases, when additional men were wanted, handfuls of tickets were thrown out among the eager and struggling crowd, and he who was fortunate enough in the scramble to secure one of these was provided with a half day's labour. In others, a foreman stationed at the dock gates, secured the men he desired by scanning the throng and pointing to one and to another who seemed most capable of hard labour, or in most need. It was a sad and distressing social sight.

London Shipping Lines

The development of the greatest docks complex in London resulted in the establishment of many shipping lines. The "Bibby Line" was the first founded by John Bibby in 1807, followed by the "Ben Line" in 1825, the "City Line" in 1840 and the "Harrison Line" in 1853. Each line adopted a method of naming its ships - the Ben Line after Scottish peaks (e.g. 'Benleuch'); the Bibby Line after English country shires (e.g. 'Lancashire'); the Ellerman City Line after cities on its trade route (e.g. 'City of Johannesburg' in its South African trade); and the Harrison Line after trades and professions (e.g. 'Philosopher').

The Bibby Line's vessels plied in the Burma and Ceylon routes from the 1880s to the beginning of World War II, bringing teak and ores from Burma, and rubber and tea from Ceylon. Once the war ended, Britain began to withdraw from her empire and trade which had followed the flag also had to withdraw.

In 1859, the Ben Line despatched a ship to China and Japan which took two years. The Line had much success in the tea trades with these two countries and soon their new steamships were calling at Yokohama, Kobe, Shang-Hai, Hong Kong, Singapore and Penang, opening up the Far Eastern market. Early in the 20th century the Ben Line directed its Far East vessels to the Import Dock of the West India Dock and for many years these vessels brought a substantial quantity of tea, as well as rubber, copra, rice, hemp and timber. Harrison Line's London-West Indies service began in 1920 and continued until 1978, during which time its ships also discharged in the Import Dock, bringing sugar, rum, molasses and fine hardwoods.

The Ellerman City Line formed in 1901 and traded with East and South Africa for many years bringing a commodity which strained industrial relations - hides. These came as wet or dry and the dockers had a name for each kind. Wet hides were 'stinkers' (justifiably!) and 'dirty money' had to be negotiated for each separate consignment of this obnoxious cargo as all parcels contaminated the handlers' clothes. Dry hides were 'empty bullocks', but these posed only a minor problem, since claims for 'anthrax money' could never be substantiated.

The year 1987 marked the 150th anniversary of the beginning of the Peninsular and Oriental Steam Navigation Company, known today as the P & O. It was founded in August 1837 by two ship owners, McGhie Wilcox and Arthur Anderson, to carry mail to Spain and Portugal. Earlier in 1835 they chartered the 206-ton William Fawcett to open the first regular mail service and she is regarded as the first P & O liner. In 1844, they started operating cruises to Malta, Athens, Rhodes, Jaffa and Egypt. Later this was extended to Norway.

3/12/37 11

THE BEN LINE  **STEAMERS Ltd.**

FOR

STRAITS, PHILIPPINES, CHINA, & JAPAN.

WITH LIBERTY TO CALL AT OTHER PORTS

ALSO TAKING CARGO FOR USUAL TRANSHIPMENT PORTS

STEAMERS	FOR	CLOSING DATES.			
		LEITH	ANTWERP	M'BRO	LONDON
X Benlawers	Penang, Port Swettenham, Malacca, Singapore, Hong Kong.	—	—	10 Dec.	17 Dec,
Benvenue	Port Said, Penang, Port Swettenham, Singapore, MANILA, Hong Kong, Nagasaki, Moji, Kobe, Osaka and Yokohama.	—	17 Dec.	24 Dec.	31 Dec.
Bencruachan	Port Said*, Penang, Port Swettenham, Singapore and Hong Kong.	—	—	7 Jan.	14 Jan.
Benavon	Port Said*, Penang, Port Swettenham, Singapore, MANILA, Hong Kong, Nagasaki, Kobe, Osaka and Yokohama.	—	14 Jan.	21 Jan.	28 Jan.
Bengloe	Port Said*, Penang, Port Swettenham Malacca, Singapore and Hong Kong.	—	—	4 Feb.	11 Feb.
Benvorlich	Port Said*, Penang, Port Swettenham, Singapore, MANILA, Hong Kong, Nagasaki, Moji, Kobe, Osaka and Yokohama.	4 Feb.	11 Feb.	18 Feb.	25 Feb.
Benarty	Port Said*, Penang, Port Swettenham, Singapore and Hong Kong.	—	—	4 Mar.	11 Mar.
Benwyvis	Port Said*, Penang, Port Swettenham, Singapore, MANILA, Hong Kong, Nagasaki, Kobe, Osaka and Yokohama.	4 Mar.	11 Mar.	18 Mar.	25 Mar

X REFRIGERATOR SPACE.

*Through Bills/Lading issued for Cairo.

SHANGHAI Cargo accepted with option of transhipment.

Sailings from HULL if sufficient inducement.

London Loading Berth-WEST INDIA DOCK

N.B.—All quotations & bookings are made subject to Steamers, space and labour being available

LAND CARGO.—The Owners and Brokers will accept no responsibility for delivering B/L to Shippers on application, unless Suppliers instruct them to the contrary before shipment of goods

DANGEROUS CARGO—S ppers' attention is drawn to the requirements of the Merchant Shipping Acts, and to the necessity of communicating with loading brokers before dispatch.

FOR FREIGHT APPLY TO

Wm. THOMSON & CO., LEITH, Managers.

T. A. BULMER & CO., LTD., MIDDLESBRO.
OUGHTRED & HARRISON, Ltd. HULL
W. T. MITCHELL & CO. MANCHESTER
BENJN. ACKERLEY & SON, BRADFORD.
KELLER, BRYANT & Co.. SOUTHAMPTON.

A. BULCKE & CO. (Succrs.), ANTWERP.
MENZELL & Co., G.m.b.h., HAMBURG.
MEYER & CO.'S SHIPPING CO., Ltd. ROTTERDAM
G. FERON, E. de CLEBSATTEL & CIE, PARIS:
A. P. de BORVILLE-MOREL DUNKIRK

KILLICK MARTIN & Co., *Brokers,*

7 Fen Court, Fenchurch Street, London, E.C.

Bills of Lading can be obtained of G. W. DRAY & SON Ltd., 34 Lime Street E.C., and P. H. GOSLIN & Co., 2 Jewry Street, E.C.3.

Telephone Nos.—Mansion House 3391 (7 lines) Telegraphic Address Kilmart, Fen, London

A shipping list prepared by the Ben Line Shipping Company showing the vessels, loading ports and respective dates in 1937.

Sir Samuel Cunard.

Thomas and James Harrison.

Alexander and William Thomson.

BRITANNIA – 1840.

PHILOSOPHER – 1857.

Sir Edmund Vestey.

WILLIAM FAWCETT - 1835

HERDSMAN – 1947

Sir John Ellerman.

THAMES SHIPBUILDING - 1910

SCOTTISH STAR - 1985

Arthur Anderson, founder of P&O

Founders of Shipping Lines Sir Samuel Cunard, founder of Cunard Steam Ship Company and their first ship "the Britannia". The Scottish brothers Thomas and James Harrison, founders of the Harrison Line with their ships "The Philosopher" and "Herdsman". Alexander and William Thomson founders of the Ben Line. Sir John Ellerman, founder of the Ellerman Line. Sir Edmund Vestey, founder of the Blue Funnel Line and one of their later ships "Scottish Blue Star". Arthur Anderson, joint founder of the P & O Line and their first ship the paddle steamer "William Fawcett". The bottom left picture shows a ship building scene along the Thames, c1910.

The P & O had a group of companies operating to different parts of the world, including the Union Line and Strick Line, which operated services to the Persian Gulf. In 1987 P & O acquired European Ferries providing a service across the English Channel to Europe. Today P & O Containers Limited operate at PLA's Northfleet Hope Terminal in Tilbury Docks, linking Europe with Australia and New Zealand, East and South Africa, the Middle East, India and the Far East, and the USA.

The Cunard Steam Ship Company was formed in 1830 by Sir Samuel Cunard and in the early 1920s acquired Brocklebank and Port Line. Daniel Brocklebank built his first ships in Whitehaven in 1770. Cunard had been carrying cargo on its passenger ships since 1840, but it was not until the company's acquisition of Port Line that cargo operations began to operate separately. The "QE2", launched in 1969, was the first Cunard vessel designed without freight facility. In 1971 the Company was taken over by the Trafalgar House Group and its containerised cargo handling has expanded.

In 1909 the Blue Star Line was formed by Sir Edmund Vestey specialising in refrigerated cargoes which operated services to New Zealand in 1931 and to Australia in 1934. For nearly half a century frozen meat was discharged in the Royal Victoria and Albert Docks. Large quantities of beef were shipped from Sir Edmund's estates in South America.

Port of London Authority 1909

Early 20th Century

By the end of the 19th century a crisis had arisen in the Port of London almost comparable to that at the end of the 18th. The continued growth of the steamship was such that the shallow river approach and difficulties of navigation had become a serious handicap and the up river docks were mainly being used for warehousing with access by lighter. There were complaints of insufficient facilities, poor rail communications, slow turnaround and exorbitant dock charges.

In 1799 a Parliamentary committee had outlined the future form of the Port. The Royal Commission of 1900 recommended in a somewhat similar fashion that a single authority should administer the river from Teddington to the sea. Both docks, river and estuary would be under a single control and thus more resources could be brought to bear to improve the seaway to London. Through the Thames Conservancy Act of 1905 a new era opened and hence forward the policy was to construct deeper channels aligned to make the most use of tidal scout rather than just to carry out remedial dredging operations. A Bill to establish the Port of London Authority was promised by King Edward VII in his speech at the opening of Parliament in 1903 but the formation of a public enterprise to acquire so much dock property seemed a threat of socialism and it was not until December 1908 that the Port of London Act became law.

A painting of the Surrey Commercial Docks at the time of the formation of the Port of London Authority in 1909 is shown on page 4. A quarter of the forest products entering the United Kingdom came through these docks. Four separate companies combined in 1864 to form the Surrey Commercial Dock Company. By 1901 the docks were at their peak. Note the huge stacks of stored timber, some were 30 ft high, handled by PLA porters. The floating timber in the ponds was handled by PLA "Rafters" who moved the floating timber with spiked poles.

Left: (a) Bustling activities at Limehouse Dock by Gustav Doré, c1870s. (b) The West India Import Dock crowded with ships discharging cargoes of sugar, rum, coffee and molasses from the West Indies, c1880s.
Right: (c) Millwall Central Granary built at Millwall Inner Dock early 1900s. (d) Irongate Wharf next to Tower Bridge, c1904. (e) Blackwall and Bugsby Reach of the Thames looking south towards Woolwich c1880s.

The new Authority took on a lot of development work but this was halted during the First World War. The thriving conditions that prevailed in the docks immediately after prompted the PLA to extend the Albert Dock by the construction of the King George V Dock which opened in July 1921 at a cost of £4½m and it was able to accommodate the largest liners of up to 30,000 tons. This was virtually the end of major dock building in the area.

Port Operation

Physically the port consisted of 69 miles of the tidal Thames and five great dock systems with 36 miles of deep-water quays equipped to deal with the huge volume of traffic flowing in and out. Hundreds of riverside wharves ancillary to, but in a great many cases competing with the docks, and a large number of riverside industries, added to it's facilities and business.Linking docks, wharves, power stations, oil installations, factories and the hinterland served by canals and tributaries, were 7,000 tugs and barges which transported much of the cargo. In the background stood the commodity markets and a vast population within a short radius of the Capital.

Generally, dockers discharged ships and handled cargo on the quayside, in transit sheds or warehouses, whilst stevedores were employed on ship discharge and all loading operations. The transit sheds were adjacent to a loading or discharging berth and were usually of single storey construction. These were used for the temporary storage of imports prior to delivery. Equally, they received exports which were stowed to port marks before delivery to ship's side. Situated between the ship and the shed was the quay forming a working area forcargo to and from the ship's side. The warehouses were generally brick built and contained more than one floor for the long term storage of cargo on behalf of merchants.

To meet the requirements of the Port for the movement of goods and passengers within the port, certain dockers were appointed as Licensed Watermen and Lightermen. The Watermen and Lightermen's Company was brought into existence by an Act of Parliament in 1555 to exercise control over the River Thames. In order to qualify for the job, men were required to be apprenticed to a Freeman of the Company of Watermen and Lightermen for a period of seven years, normally completing training at the age of 21. The Lightermen were then employed in river tugs under experienced skippers. Some tugs were owned by Lighterage companies.

Left: (a) North Quay of London Docks, c1890s. (b) Horse Tram at the West India Station, c1910. (c) Wine Gauging on the North Quay of London Docks, c1890s. (d) Billingsgate Fish Market early 1900s.
Right: (e) The impressive old entrance to the East India Docks at Blackwall, c1880s. (f) The old gateway of the West India Dock, 1920s. Sadly, both entrances were demolished early in the 20th century to provide access for modern transport.

While the original dock companies were protected by their period of monopoly and enjoyed the rare privilege of having their own bonded warehouses, the "free water clause" as it became called , was of no great consequence. After these monopolies expired and the Government adopted a Free Trade policy, the docks faced increasing competition from private wharfingers. The "free water clause" came to be inserted in every dock Act and the companies were compelled to watch their dividends shrink as lighters passed in and out through their lock gates free of charge and without hindrance. Even the opening of Tilbury Docks gave further scope for the lighterage industry ferrying goods to London.

This situation gave the Port of London its peculiar - perhaps unique - character. Until the 1970s a popular visual image of the Port had been a London tug with its train of loaded lighters. These lighters would probably have been coming from a dock, down river, where they would have been loaded directly over the side of a ship. They would be going up river to one of the many warehouses, which, until the recent extensive demolition, used to line much of the river from the Lower Pool to Westminster and beyond. Competition from riverside wharves as well as between the docks themselves induced amalgamation of the independent companies that had originally built the docks.

Officers of HM Customs and Excise controlled the landing and shipping of merchandise and examined cargoes. They were stationed at a great number of small offices throughout the docks and wharves. Also in each control there was a Port Health Officer who worked under the direction of an Administrator of the City of London. He examined all the various types of cargo taking samples and forwarding them to laboratories for examination.

Left: (1) Repairing a ship's propeller in the dry dock of King George V Dock, 1930. (2) A Trinity House Pilot boarding a ship in the Thames taking over from the Pilot based at Gravesend, 1946. (3) Thames sailing barges at the entrance lock of Greenland Dock in the Surrey Commercial Docks, 1930 (4) Sailing barges at Southwark Corporation's Greenmoor Wharf refuse depot at Bankside, c1930. Right: (5) One of the jetties for the discharge of coal at Beckton Gas Works, which was the largest in the world, 1922. (6) Ships discharging timber into the quayside and into lighters at the Canada Dock in the Surrey Docks, 1930s. (7) Unloading wool bales on the North Quay of the Import Dock of the West India Docks, 1950s. (8) The newly completed Ford Motor Works on the Thames at Dagenham which was the largest in the UK, 1933. (9) The City of London Corporation's Port Health Authority launch the "Howard Deighton", early 1930s. All incoming ships were checked by the Port medical officers for infectious diseases. (10) Carcasses of lamb being discharged into quayside of the Royal Albert Dock, c1930.

About 15 million tons of goods passed through the enclosed docks during the year, half of which passed over the quays. The value of these goods was so large that their custody demanded the utmost vigilance. The PLA therefore maintained from their own revenue a special police force in the docks of about 600 employees. On the other hand, the river and river wharves were looked after by the Metropolitan Police who were a common sight on the tideway. Each dock group was fenced and all gates were manned by constables who checked the traffic through. The docks were patrolled throughout the night and the force had a Criminal Investigation Department to investigate any crime committed on PLA premises. The police knew when vehicles would be loaded at the various sheds and they would man the sheds up accordingly.

The London District Pilotage was in five main sections; Cinque Ports, the North Channel, the Channel, the compulsory River Thames and the Medway. Assuming that it was a foreign going vessel, the River Thames Pilot would take over at Gravesend and attend to its arrangements. Depending on the size of the ship, a tug would be at hand and go all the way up river and assist with the berthing. A pilot first got a license after working for three years to a draught of 14 ft. It was really their learning time before sitting for the examinations at Trinity House. The license was only good for a year and the Pilot would re-sit the examination every year. They had to learn all the depths, buoys, marks and the banks, and the tides in and out, as well as the berths along the river. The handling of ships in the docks was performed by the Dockmaster's staff.

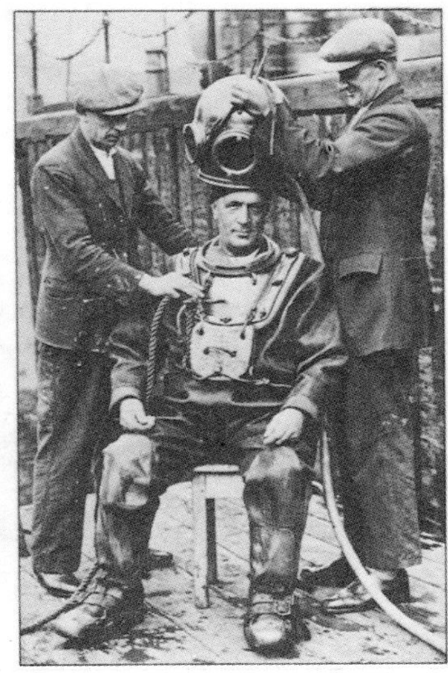

Left: (1) Dockers loading bags of sugar from the Caribbean into the North Quay Warehouses at the West India Import Dock, 1930. (2) Senior Captain Latta of the Canadian Pacific Steamship Company at the Surrey Commercial Docks, 1930.
(3) Weighing and sorting ivory tusks at the London Docks, 1930.
Middle: (4) Customs officials inspecting bales of cinnamon at London Docks Warehouses, 1930. (5) An electric platform truck for handling cargo at the Royal Docks, 1920s. (6) A PLA diver preparing for a salvage operation, 1930s.
Right: (7) Ship's painters swing precariously on boson's' chairs while working on a funnel, 1930s. (8) A dock policeman searching, or 'rubbing down' a docker at the gates. 16ft high walls surrounded all the docks to provide security for cargo stored in the warehouses and transit sheds, 1900.
(9) Stevedores loading a lighter (barge) from overside a Brocklebank ship, destined for the river wharves of the Port, c1930s.
(10) Irongate Wharf and St Katharine Wharf adjacent to Tower Bridge, c1937. These were operated by the General Steam Navigation Company, which ran regular services to European Ports until the 1960s. Just to the north of the wharves were the St Katharine warehouses. On this site the Tower Thistle Hotel was built in 1973.

London Industry and Trade 1920s and 1930s
The Great Market and Finance Centre of the World

Port of London 1920s

From the early 1920s, most work in the docks had been paid for at piece rate. Knowing that their output and thus their earnings would seldom be eroded by having to 'carry' unenthusiastic casual workers in their gangs, the permanent labourers worked hard and regularly took home good wages. One very acceptable benefit of this state of affairs was considerably better than average industrial relations. Evening football matches between dock staff and its permanent labourers were ample proof of this and several shipping companies became so keen to have their ships discharged in the Royal docks that they would hold them in the river until berths became available. Under the control of the PLA the business of the docks expanded enormously. Annually £49million worth of merchandise passed through giving an idea of the magnitude of its commerce. The value of sterling of the total foreign trade of the port rose from £322m in 1909 to approx. £740m in 1925.

International Market

The trade of the port was in reality a reflection of the trade of the United Kingdom. The capital did not develop into a large port because of the needs of the Londoners, although within a 25 mile radius there was a population of some 9 million people. There were also in and around London engineering works, clockmakers, biscuit manufacturers, furniture factories, breweries, tobacco works and so on. London had developed into a great international market and financial centre of the world. An enormous proportion of its population found their vocation as distributors and middlemen, financiers and bankers, bookkeepers and clerks. Immense quantities of goods were imported not only for the population to consume or manufacture, but for storage and distribution to other parts of the kingdom and to many parts of the world.

The warehousing of goods formed a large part of the business of the port. When goods were landed on the dock quays which were mostly covered by transit sheds, the port authority took charge of them, some being placed directly onto railway trucks or road vehicles for conveyance to their destination, while others were taken into one or other of the warehouses pending their being required for home delivery or export. The port of London was therefore something more than a dock operation undertaking. They had a vast range of warehouses and in addition to handling nearly 2½million tons of imported, and 800,000 tons of export goods every year, they had entrusted to their care a stock of over ½million tons of merchandise. These warehouses were a great advantage to merchants who did not wish to receive all of the consignments on arrival.

Bonded Warehouses

The bonded warehouses, where dutiable goods were stored, were of special value to importers as duties payable on certain goods constituted by far the greater portion of their value. Some goods, particularly spirits, often remained in store for a considerable time, and the amount of importer's money tied up if duty had to be paid at time of landing would have been very large. The authority performed many intricate and expert operations on behalf of the merchants and importers, such as reporting on weight & condition, sorting the produce to quality marks, opening the packages for inspection and sale, as well as furnishing samples to represent the exact condition of the produce or article. The extent of the work done in the port can be judged by the fact that their employees numbered about 10,000 of whom half were of the class known as dock labourers. The total number of persons employed by the port authority including administrative was over 12,000.

Some description of the principal commodities dealt with in the docks and warehouses and the special facilities provided for them is of interest. Grain, sugar, tobacco, meat and soft fruit formed the bulk of the tonnage, but innumerable other articles were dealt with. Goods arrived from all parts of the world including mahogany from British Honduras, Cuba, Costa Rica and Africa, Cedar from Honduras and Mexico; walnut, rosewood, ebony and teak from India, Asia and America; costly carpets from India, Turkey, and China; silks from India, China and Japan; porcelain from China and Japan; idols, ivory figures, bronzes and cabinets from the Orient; furs from Canada and Russia, marble from Italy and Asia Minor, rubber from India, Colombo, Java and Singapore; shells from the southern seas; Ivory from Africa and India; feathers from Africa's golden sand; spices from Ceylon as well as all the perfumes of Arabia!

When the London and St Katharine docks were built they were accessable to all vessels then afloat. During the 1920s and 30s the ocean-going ship was too large to enter these docks and they were only used for steamers of moderate size, usually those engaged in coasting and near continental trades. The warehouses although rather old, were most substantial so that large quantities of goods imported into the other modern docks were brought to them for storage. Chief among these goods was wool, which required a very large area of nearly 1m sq.ft for its accommodation. Wines and spirits demanded a storage space of nearly 650,000 sq.ft. There were also other commodities which were the most valuable products in the port of London. They embraced drugs, iodine, gums, ivory, tortoise-shell, quicksilver, coffee, and dried and canned foods.

Rubber Imports

In view of the rapid growth of rubber imports for the car industry the port authority found it necessary to devote considerably more space than formerly to this valuable commodity. Extensive premises were provided on the north side of the Western London Dock. Three single storey sheds furnished with ample overhead lighting, were at the service of the trade for the preliminary operations connected with the examination of rubber on its arrival. The operations performed by the authority included weighing, tarring, sorting to qualities and grades. Samples were also drawn, sealed and forwarded to the selling brokers who submitted them to the Rubber Trade Associations standard quality prospective buyers. After the goods had been thus worked and inspected, they were repacked and stored to avoid deterioration which could ensue from exposure to light. London was a principal market in the world for rubber with over 70,000 tons being dealt with anually.

Pearl and Tortoise-shell

Another interesting warehouse "I" at St Katharine dock was partly occupied by scent and perfume. Imported extracts of flowers were mixed with fat, and on arrival these were separated from the fat by special machinery and then mixed with alcohol. Equally exotic were the rooms set aside for shells where valuable mother of pearl was viewed beneath a special skylight. Tortoise-shell from the West Indies was much in evidence and became more expensive as demand increased.

The Great Wool Sales

Steamers carried wool from Australia and New Zealand to the Royal Docks for transfer to the London or St Katharine Docks. The Wool Warehouses had huge floors with flying bridges running across from one to another. By the time the wool entered the warehouse it was marked in red or black ink or with the initials of the ship. A one pound sample would be extracted and sent off to the broker or merchant. At warehouses in London Docks, 19 acres of floor space were available for the storage of 40,000 bales of wool, and special show floors at the top of the warehouses were set apart for the display of wool to prospective buyers. About 18,000 bales could be shown at any one time. On the day of the sales, buyers came to the warehouses armed with catalogues. They wore white overalls to avoid soiling their clothes with the grease in the wool. and walked along the gangways between the bales. The buyers were men from the mills of Yorkshire or the West Country; Americans came from Boston; the Flemish from Antwerp; Germans from Chemmitz or Blumenthal. By noon most of the buyers had finished their inspections and the warehouse gangs had taken over to stuff the protruding portions used as samples, back into the bales.

Dockside Scenes and Busy Wharves
Top: (a) Dockyard workers sifting sugar into sacks in the North Quay Warehouses of the West India Import Dock, 1930. (b) Shipping in the Upper Pool attracts the attention of City workers, c1930. The busy wharves and warehouses that lined the City and Southwark riverbank remained active with shipping and lighters until the container revolution of the late 1960s.
Centre: (a) More bananas than flat caps in this photograph, a new shipment of fruit is being loaded onto trains at Canary Wharf for Covent Garden Market, 1930. (b) The wine gauging ground and North Quay of the London Docks, Wapping, 1920. Here many thousands of barrels of wine, sherry and port were stored for sampling and gauging before being consigned to the labyrinth of vaults that lay below.
Bottom: (a) Dockers at the Dock Labour Board Office in the Royal Docks, 1950s. (b) The giant liner "Dominion Monarch" in the dry dock of the King George V Dock, towers above the streets of Silvertown in 1950. Spectacular sights like this were once common in the lower docks. Growing up in the shadow of ships, many children would find eventual employment in the docks or on the riverside as their parents had done.

The actual sales took place six times a year at the Wool Exchange in Coleman Street, each sale lasting several weeks. In the Auction Room, the proceedings went forward at extreme speed with some lots knocked down at the rate of five or six a minute. The auctioneer called out the number of the lot and often added the minimum price demanded. Within a day or so after the close of the daily Sales, the bales would leave by lorries or trains, or go into the holds of ships for export to other countries all over the world.

African Ivory and Eastern Spices

The main entrance to the London Docks was off a cobbled street which lead to a broad road widening into an open space where hundreds of casks of wine lying on the stones were being attended to by gaugers and samplers. A short distance further along on the right the No.6 Warehouse displayed a sign "Entrance to the Ivory, Cinnamon, Spice and Bark Floors".

Within this building were stores of eastern spices, barks and the tusks of elephants from Africa and Asia with big wine vaults in the basement. The ground floor was the centre of the world's supply of ivory with over ten thousand elephant tusks lying there, some of which could weigh over 200 pounds and measure 12 ft. On arrival in packages of one or two, the tusks were immediately examined by the experts for any damage. If a crack was observed, two parallel lines were placed beside the fault and two wavy marks if the flow was a long one. The colour of the tusks displayed on the floor varied from yellowish brown to dark colours. Tusks from Congo and Sudan were darker than those from Zanzibar; small milk tusk shed by young elephants had a lighter colour with the occasional hunters' bullet mark visible. Occasionally the tusks of mammoths (fossil ivory) dug up in Siberia arrived at the warehouse, the surface looked like wood and was brown in colour. Stacked in barrels at one end of the Ivory Floor, one could also see small tusks from whales and teeth from hippopotamus and walrus.

On the first floor of the No 6 Warehouse you would wonder at the Eastern delights of spices. They arrived in London to the tune of 20,000 tons a year and most of it was stored in this floor. Each of the three upper floors spices, barks and cinnamon was a huge area with iron shelving with stacks of boxes, bags, mats and bundles of all shapes. Nutmegs came in mahogany "Singapore boxes" painted black at the edges. Cinnamon was in bales. The men on this floor spent their time mainly sampling and grading the spice products and separating the good from the damaged.

In addition to pepper and nutmegs, there were capsicums, cloves, chillies, carsmons, cassia, cinnamon, ginger, mace and pimento. The capsicums looked like dried pea pods, red in hue, the smaller sorts were called "cherries". Cloves, dried flower buds from Penang and Zanzibar look like small nails. Cassia, emanating from the brown strips of bark, had a pleasing odour and was used for incense. Cinnamon bark in rolledup dried sticks about 18 inches long. While a lot of the products from these floors were used by the housewives in their kitchens, a substantial amount emerged from No 6 Warehouse for medical uses.

Meat at the Royals

The meat was kept in Z and A sheds of the Victoria Dock. These were open berths - no four walls here, with gantries running along with hooks and chains to hold the sides of beef. All the meat vans would be backed along the bank and as dockers discharged the meat from the holds of various ships the different merchants would have their representatives present to mark up their vans as to the meat they wanted, such as Armours, Swifts, Fatstocks. The merchants representatives would hire lorries Union Cartage, Hays Wharf, etc. and the dockers who discharged the ships. In the refrigerated ships the meat would be stowed in different cupboards for each merchant. One would be filled for instance for Armour, then the doors would be closed as it was refrigerated by the ships engines, and another cupboard might contain Fatstocks.

The meat used to be put on the chain and one man was especially employed to push it along for Customs inspection , weighing, etc., to see if it complied with all the rules and regulations. Custom Officers did not specialise; they dealt with all kinds of cargoes. The dockers would still be working while the Custom officers were inspecting one or two packages out of a couple of hundred. Sometimes they got a Bill of Lading for cargo and they would ask for special numbers. Say it was curios, the Custom Officers would ask for the A in a diamond. So the men found 'A in a diamond', and if cases were numbered, he might then say he would like to inspect number 62. The PLA staff would have to dig it out, put it in a special cage for customs then open up the contents and lay them out for inspection. Subsequently, they were packed up and marked with chalk "HMC"; so everybody knew it has been opened for Customs. The meat, such as beef, lamb, offal and port, came from South America and the Argentine. The carcasses would be landed on a bogey and driven away from the side of the ship to the vans. So if dockers had a load of Armour's beef, they went to where the Armour vans were on the bank, and the merchant would chalk up the grade of beef he wanted and its destination. The dockers would load the vans, filled with ice to keep it cold and they would go off to various shops and depots around London including Spitalfields market. The meat was wrapped in white cloth and over that a sacking which was marked Armours, or Swifts, or Smithfield or Fatstocks.

Wine in London Docks

In the London Docks the wine and spirit trade flourished. Many times at 15 vaults the coopers would prepare some 340450 wine casks for `allround' gauging in one day. This would be from 8am to 7pm and would involve perhaps six or seven Customs Officers. Casks would be prepared so that they were 'sound', not leaking, no hoops missing. The coopers would also have to release the `bung' (shive) with a wooden tool called a 'flogger'. Using a scribing iron they would proceed to cut into the casks heads, this would give such information as the ship's rotation number (each ship on passing a certain point on the River Thames is given a number, Merchant's name and custom's numbers). When the Customs Officer had finished gauging, he would then scribe on the contents and the ullage (ullage meaning the actual amount of wine in the cask). Whilst loading and unloading the dockers would use 'Can-Hooks' which they would fit on the end of the cask (or the 'Chime').

HM Custom's Wine Gauging

The term used of 'gauging' a cask was the system by which the capacity of vats, casks and other vessels, and the quantity of liquid they contained, were ascertained from dimensions taken by means of a measuring instrument. The content was the capacity of a cask. Vacuity was the difference between the bung diameter and the 'wet' inches, also the difference between the content and the liquid ullage quantity (in other words the empty portion of a cask). Another example of this word 'ullage' was the amount by which a cask or container vessel was less than full through evaporation, leakage etc.

The vaults were important because wines and spirits from all over the world were generally loaded from the Royal Docks and West India docks, into craft and sent there. Some went by road, and this was then dispatched to London docks. Whenever they left the ships, the wines and spirits were always placed in bonded craft or bonded vehicle for dispatch. They were under Customs lock and there was generally a Customs-watcher accompanying the goods.

The Coopers

The coopers used a tin patch for temporary repairs perhaps to a missing or damaged stave and once ashore a new stave would be fitted to the cask. They worked in the ship's hold as well as on the quayside. The most vivid memory dockers and coopers had from the docks was the overpowering smell of rum, molasses, limejuice, and many others, such as spices, sugar etc. They believed this aroma stayed with them forever.

Vanished Scenes at Butlers Wharf

Left: (a) The old Butlers Wharf at Shad Thames, next to Tower Bridge, which became famous for handling tea and other commodities. Today it has been converted into luxury apartments and offices. (b) Office staff in the 1930s. (c) Discharge of tea chests from barges and (d) weighing and grading of teas in the warehouse.
Middle: (a) Cutting tobacco leaves, (b) dockers waiting to be taken on, (c) wine gauging on the quayside, and (d) preparing tea chests for weighing.
Right:(e) Busy unloading along the quayside, (f) dockers wages collection counter,
(g) dockers moving cargo into warehouses and (h) young boys labelling tins of tea under the watchful eye of the supervisor!

Tour of The Royal Victoria Dock 1936

The entrance to the Royal Victoria Dock was by way of the "Engineers' Gate". Across to the left the "A" Berth was the home of the Blue Star boats, "Avila Star" and her sister ships. The "A" Berth was almost unique in its handling of chilled meat; from the ships it would be discharged onto electric bogies called "doodlebugs", busy but harmless little battery driven trucks, then placed onto an overhead conveyor system to waiting vehicles. Each piece was individually labeled with the address of a shop and went straight from ship to shop in less than 24 hours.

Walking along the dock in a westerly direction the feature distinguishing the "Vic" from most other docks could be seen. The quay, lined with old brick warehouses, had jetties arranged at right angles; some stone and some with wooden decking, had either corrugated iron or brick built sheds on them. The tobacco warehouse "M" was separated from the dock by a quay barely ten feet wide. The two largest jetties were the home of the Japanese "Maru" boats. Further along, at one of the smaller jetties, the Royal Mail ships "Culebra" and "Lombardy", could be seen. The last berth in the dock on this northern side was "Z" Shed, built on similar lines to the one at "A" Berth. The famous "Highland" boats, with their squat twin funnels, shared this shed with the equally distinctive Houlder Line ships, which bore a white Maltese cross on their dark red and black funnels.

Along the south side of the dock, the first three sheds were the most modern. The quay also had "highflyer" electric cranes the only area to be so equipped in the whole dock. The buff funneled ships of the PSN Line from such ports as Valparaiso and Santiago de Chile called here. Beyond this, was a large complex of flour mills whose tall chimneys poured an endless stream of thick black smoke across the dock. At the "dolphins" in front of the mills, tramp steamers from all over the world discharged their grain into giant silos. The ships were usually surrounded by floating grain elevators, unloading the golden cargo into barges. These huge elevators, each with two funnels, made a peculiar hollow puffing noise as they worked like giant vacuum cleaners sucking the grain up from the ship's hold and sending it into waiting craft, where it was trimmed into pyramids by the "toe rags" as the PLA grain porters were known. On the opposite side of the dock was the entrance to the Graving Dock, a large sheet of water, the further side of which was occupied by a timber yard and wharf. This basin was known as the "Pontoon Dock" by older people in the area for many years ago it was the site of an elaborate device for raising ships onto pontoons to enable repairs to be carried out to their underwater portions. Although the apparatus had long since vanished, the name and the half dozen narrow inlets at each end of the dock still survived.

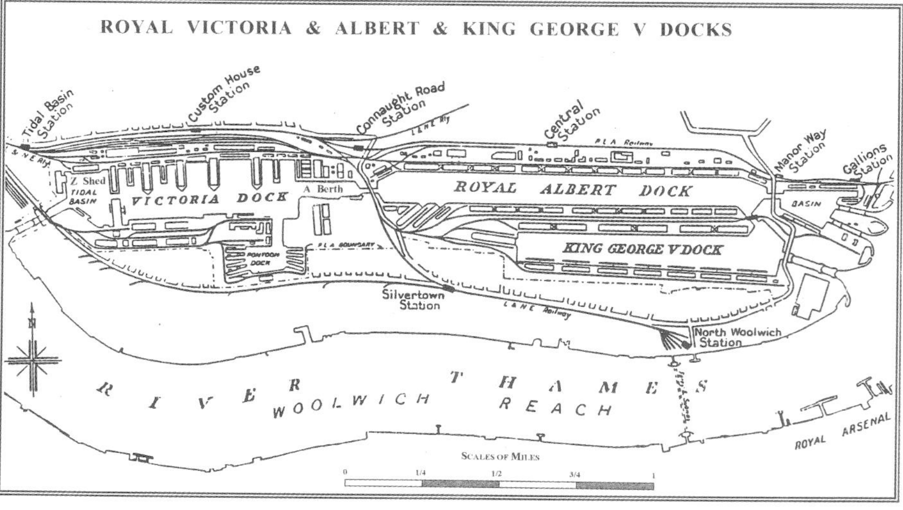

(a) The 1934 season of the Port of London Authority's River and Dock Cruises started on 6 December with a trip from the Tower Pier. This picture taken from the touring steamer as it was towed through the Albert Dock by a tug. (b) The Royal Victoria Dock had four solid piers built on the north side. In the foreground is the Graving Dock with flour mills in course of construction, c1933. (c) Map of The Royal Victoria Dock, c1927.

World War II and The Blitz

By the middle of the 1930s, the West India Import Dock's traffic had increased until vessels trading with all continents except Australia were regular arrivals. This pattern was not broken until the outbreak of World War II in 1939. Soon after this country became involved US vessels bringing military equipment, shells, bombs and explosives, were mostly directed to the Import Dock for urgent discharge. Those were anxious days for dock officers who, knowing that air raids were likely to begin at any moment and without warning, concentrated their best efforts on turning round the special carriers as quickly as possible, as well as other ships bringing much needed food.

With the recent 50th Anniversary of the Victory in Europe it is interesting to look at the effects the war had on East London. The main air attack by some 400 bombers came on the afternoon of Sunday 7th September, 1940 in an attempt to destroy the docks. During this raid, high explosive and incendiary bombs caused great fires in two of the Import Dock's sugar warehouses. The warehouses, which had stored large quantities of sugar consistently for 138 years, burned for nearly two days; the timber shed fires lasted nearly a week. Many ships and buildings were damaged and Londoners saw flames leaping up from various points in the densely populated districts. By 6pm the day raiders had gone but after a two-hour break the night raiding force appeared guided by the huge riverside fires which it set out to stoke with high explosive and incendiary bombs until 4am the next morning.

The whole area suffered badly during the air raids of World War 11. Around the Eastern Dock at St Katharine the Telford/Hardwick warehouses were destroyed and other warehouses in the vicinity damaged, whilst at the Surrey Commercial Docks a high proportion of the transit shed accommodation was lost. The latter was made good after the war but St Katherine's warehouses, being around a moribund dock, were never replaced. The entrance to Millwall Dock in Limehouse Reach was put out of action by the bombing and has never been rebuilt; ships entering Millwall Dock after that time took a route through the West India system using the Millwall Cut. Of the original range of eleven massive warehouses on the north quay of the West India Import Dock only warehouse No.1 and parts of Nos. 2 and 11 survived. The East India Export Dock, on the site of Brunswick Dock, was abandoned by the PLA and Brunswick Wharf power station was constructed on the site post war.

Air raids on London and its docks continued for 57 consecutive nights into early November. Throughout this exhausting experience the remaining dock workers continued to present themselves for work each day.

In both world wars, cargo and passenger ships were adapted to operate as troop carriers, hospital ships and armed cruisers. Particularly during World War II, loss of these merchant ships was very heavy. The devastating effect on shipping can be more realistically understood when it is stated that between 1939-45 the loss of shipping normally using the Port of London amounted to over four million tons.

Top: (a) Prime Minister, Neville Chamberlain, announces Britain's declaration of World War II, September 1939. (b) News vendors in front of a tree, painted white to prevent accidents during the blackouts.
Middle:(c) An artist impression of the West India and Surrey Docks under air attack during the Battle of Britain. (d) Queen Elizabeth (today the Queen Mother) visited the local people during the London Blitz on 11 September 1940.
Bottom: (e) Concrete breakwater caissons for the "Mulberry Harbour" invasion by the Allied Forces, under construction at the East India Import Dock, 1944. (f) Sir Winston Churchill inspecting war damage at the House of Commons.

The Post War Period of 1950 to 1980

After the war, repair work was carried out on the remaining dock premises in the docks and important facilities were replaced. There was also a need to overcome the upheaval in industrial relations caused by the introduction in 1947 of the government-created National Dock Labour Scheme, which made various concessions to dockers undreamed of by even the most optimistic crusaders and social workers at the turn of the century. Among other things, it abolished casual dock labour at a stroke and, in its place, guaranteed all dock labourers in the 84 biggest UK ports 'jobs for life'. It also took all disciplinary power out of the hands of the employers, making them as well as the dockers, subject to the Scheme's rules. Its effect on productivity was disastrous.

By the early 1960s trade reached a new peak. Over a hundred ships were using the Royal Docks daily and the port as a whole was handling over 65 million tons of cargo a year. Care and supervision of goods were not confined to the docks and warehouses, customs authorities kept strict control of all dutiable goods. Electric and hydraulic cranes, the most up to date at the time, were used to shift the millions of tons of cargo that passed through each year to every part of the world. One-third of timber imports came from Finland, Russia, America and the Arctic, and passed through the Surrey Docks. Nearly one million bales of wool a year were brought through London Docks. A million tons of frozen meat came into the Royals from South America, Australia and New Zealand. Manufactured goods were exported to all parts of the world, using the biggest floating crane, the London Samson.

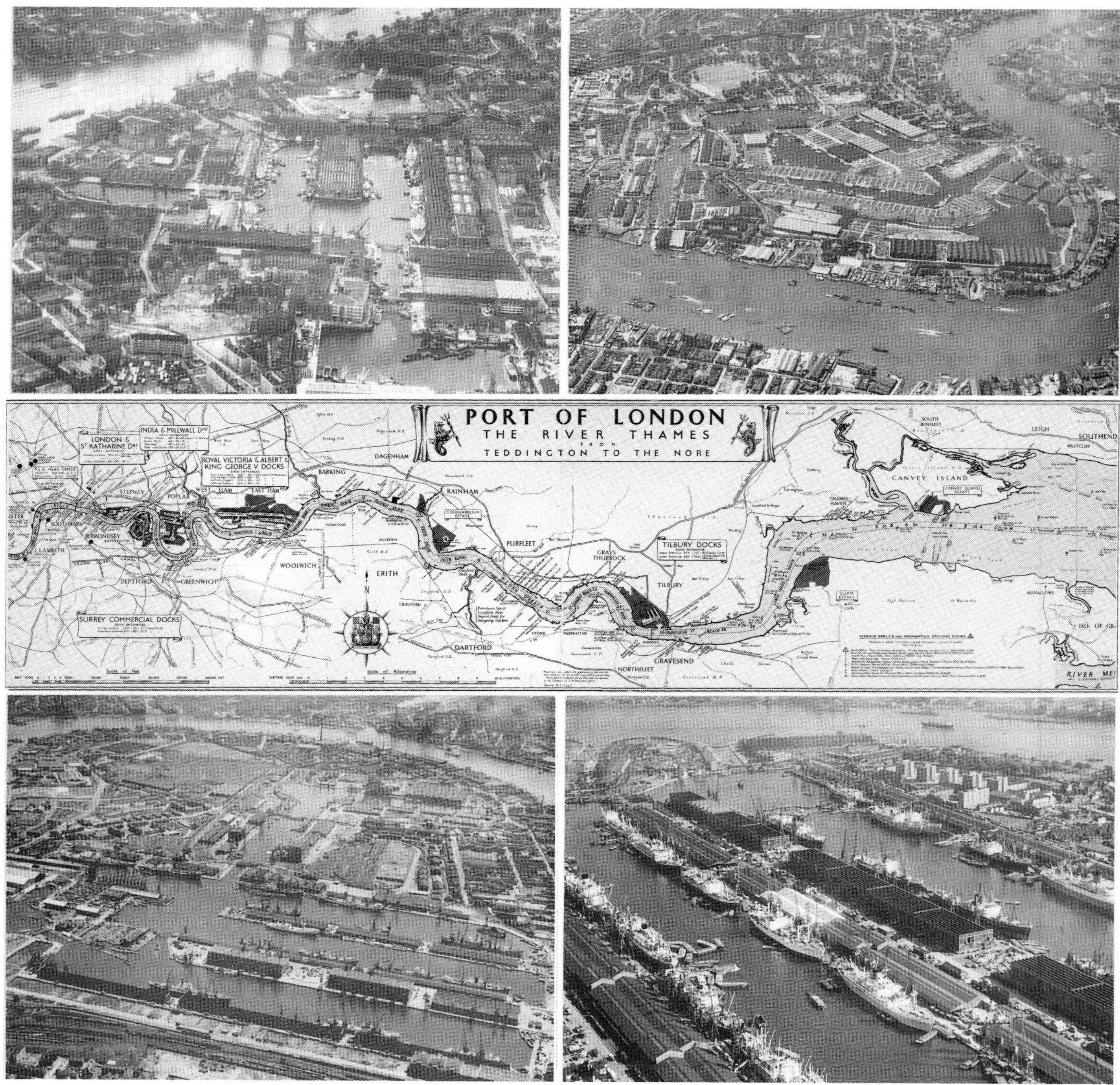

Aerial Views of London Docklands in the 1960s Top:(a) London and St Katharine Docks, the nearest to the City of London. (b) Surrey Commercial Docks on the south side of the Thames. Middle: (c) The Port of London from Teddington to the sea, 1955. Bottom: (d) India and Millwall Docks on the Isle of Dogs, looking south. Old Canary Wharf is near the bottom of the picture. (e) Royal Docks looking down on the Albert and King George V Docks.

Life and Work at the Royals

At the junction between the Royal Victoria Dock and the entrance to the Royal Albert Dock there is a very famous pub called the Connaught. At this place there would be thousands of men, not only would there be dockers and stevedores, there would be seamen from all over world looking for a familiar face. This is where dockers would be preparing themselves to shape up for work inside the Royal Albert Dock.

Now if you could imagine the situation where there had been a slump in shipping, and we have had many of them, and on this morning, there was a glut of shipping in and the recession has broken, there would be approximately five thousand men 'shaping up on the stones' as it was called for a job. There would be discussions going on about their experiences over the weekend, or about West Ham Football Club, how it played and the arguments to and fro. Conversation was often about horses and betting, and as 'off-track' betting was illegal, there would be Bookmaker's agents (known as Bookies Runners) on street corners ready to 'run', hence their name, if the police appeared. When betting shops were legalised gambling became easier for everybody.

Suddenly at 7.40am all this would break up, and you would see streams of men in their hundreds pouring through the gates from the Connaught into the Albert Dock. Outside the Albert Dock gate work sheets were put up showing different shipping companies workforce requirements for the day and as the dockers were 'piece-workers' they would try and shape up for the firm that had the easiest working cargo with the best rate of pay.

Facing the men would be the representatives of the firms, the foremen. The foreman of each firm would look at his watch and at exactly at 7.45am walk over to pick their 'slaves' or their 'beef' as they would refer to it at times, and then they would call out their regular gangs, Charlie's gang, Bill's gang, Taylor's gang. After they picked their gangs, this would leave what was known as 'floaters', men who did not belong to any particular firm, and they would be called to make up what was called 'scratch gangs'. That is, they were scratching around to get a gang of men together. Then the men would go over. But before they could be engaged for work, each docker and each stevedore had to present his dock registration book, which the employer's representative would take from them, and the moment he took it out of their hands they were engaged for work. Then he would tell them what ship they were going to and what dock, and what part of the dock or what shed. The docker would then make his way round to start work at eight oclock on that particular allocation of work.

Export and Import Scenes 1950s/1960s

Left: (a) British Marconi television equipment at Royal Albert Dock for transport to Canada. (b) Barges being loaded at the N shed of the South West India Dock for export to St Lucia in the West Indies. (c) A coach at the N shed destined for the former Rhodesia in Africa. Right: (d) Casks of hides in brine at the Albert Dock imported from Australia.

(e) Discharge of frozen meat in the Royal Docks. (f) New lock gates for Greenland Dock in the Surrey Commercial Docks (g) Tea chests being lifted from a ship's hold at Tilbury.

If ships winches were used, i.e. not using the quayside cranes) they would have two winch men, and if the cargo was going overside into the barges they would put four men into a barge to receive the cargo. If it was going quayside into the transit sheds, then they would have two men on the quayside handing over the cargo from the ships gangs.

Overside there would be two men on the winches and the top man (that was the phrase they used), would give all the hand signals to the winch drivers who had to draw the cargo safely out of the hold. There would be cold meat, frozen lambs mostly, and the dockers would use cargo nets, after loading the nets would be dragged out into the square of the hatch and hoisted up and taken over the side of the ship into the barge. If cartons of butter were being handled, then instead of using nets the butter would be stacked on cargo boards. If they were on a good earning job, piecework rate, with a ten hour day they could earn twenty pounds a week. If they were on meat, which was a fast pace job, they would get more. You must understand that all this time it was the norm for men to earn between £25 and £30 a week. It was a lot of money to the dockers, that would be up to 40 hour per week, 5½ days, then it went down to 5 days.

Some terrible accidents have happened on ships. One member of a gang had his throat cut in a part of a crane in one of the cables. He was suspended in the air and nearly lost his head. He was put on one sid to wait for the ambulance man to come on board. They would come down below in the ships hold with the stretcher and carry out the casualty and land him on the quayside by the ambulance. To give an idea regarding accidents, the accident rate in the Royal group of docks showed that one man in every fifteen hundred was killed each year, one man in every thousand suffered serious injury, and every man in the docks averaged four attendances in a year to the medicare centres for abrasions, cuts and fractures.

Closure of Docks 1970-80

One of the consequences of the Second World War was a revolution in the methods used for handling cargoes. In the 1960s the Port of London invested further in mechanical cargo handling. Within a short period of time there were considerable changes in shipping technology. This included the use of containers and roll-on/roll-off terminals which meant the large number of dockers were no longer necessary. Of the 30,000 dockers once employed at the Docks, only 3,000 were needed to cope with the cargo at Tilbury. Ships were no longer willing to take a day going up river to London and the docks started to close. The East India Dock closed in 1967, St Katherine's 1968 and the London and Surrey Docks in 1969. Despite some attempt to retain a group of docks upriver the West India closed finally by 1980 and the Royals in 1981. The area became derelict and a focus for public attention.

Millwall Docks and Central Granary

Top:Millwall Central Granary on the Isle of Dogs was opened in 1903 the first granary in the Port of London to deal with the Baltic trade. The 10-storey building was 30m high and could store up to 24,000 tons of grain.. Alongside the granary there were four fixed pneumatic elevators to discharge grain from ships direct to silos or to any of the granary floors. (a) The vessel Triwidden, discharging its grain, 1960. (b) The City of Yokohama was an Ellerman Line Ship and she would be on accommodation berth on the eastern side of Millwall and could be loading overside for South Africa (heavy machinery). Triwidden is completing discharging on the Central Granary. The accommodation in the barges consisted of a sleeping bunk and a coal-fired stove for heating.

Middle:(c) The Royal Mail van arrives on the vessel's last day's loading, early 1950s. Here the Post Office Supervisor is checking the number of Post Office bags into the cargo net. (d) Two stevedores ("pitch hands") and two postmen unload the mail bags into nets and scaleboards. The boards were lifted by means of hooks at each corner.

Bottom: (e) The Norwegian vessel K C Rogenes from the Port of Hangesund is being loaded with general cargo for George Town, Trinidad. The Hydraulic crane is loading from the sets outside the 'G' sheds. "Dirty cargo" of drumwork (40 gallons) received ex vehicle awaiting loading at No.2, the main hold on the ship. Drum crates of chemicals on quay and carboys (glass containers) awaiting loading at Flash Points (hazardous) on deck. The stevedores put them in sets and then loaded them on the 'tween deck (above lower hold). The uniformed PLA Shunter is waiting to bring his truck through. (f) A view inside Millwall Central Granary, early 1950s. Export cargo was delivered ex road and rail and placed in parts of the granary to accommodate the overflow of cargo for eventual loading onto ships. The wooden cartons of canned beans and other general cargo were destined for Demerara in the West Indies. Note the construction of floors with reinforced concrete beams on steel columns with timber boards.

Docklands Joint Committee 1976

Debates on the future of Docklands started in 1970 and numerous study reports were produced for redevelopment which had been the basis of public consultation. Despite considerable effort nothing constructive took place in the old docks and a shrinking population found itself isolated amongst the wide tracks of derelict land and buildings. In 1976 the Docklands Joint Committee, consisting of representatives of the five neighbouring boroughs, Newham, Southwark, Tower Hamlets, Greenwich and Lewisham, published the London Docklands Strategic Plan. The plan centred on increasing the number of jobs in manufacturing and other industries and the building of council homes. By 1979 it became clear that although some schemes had been started planned targets were not being achieved due to lack of funding. The Government of the day decided that improved progress would depend on the injection of substantial amounts of money and that a single-minded development agency would be the most suitable vehicle. Due to the divided interests of the parties involved not a great deal had been achieved by the early 1980s although some regeneration did take place along the western end of Docklands, see page 37, pre dating the formation of the London Docklands Development Corporation in 1981.

West India Docks January 1966

Past export scenes at the West India Docks February 1966 on the sites of Canary Wharf and Heron Quays. Top Left: The sequence of events shows one of the Port of London Authority heaviest floating cranes, "London Samson", handling a rail coach for Beira for onward shipment to Rhodesia (now Zimbabwe). The coach is being lifted from a trailer on the crosswall of the Export Dock. This area was used frequently for heavy-lift cargo, including cars, destined for export. The men in the background are the crew of the "Samson" working under the direction of the Dockmaster.

Middle: The coach has been lifted. In the background is the Ellerman & Wilson Line Vessel "Cavello" loading cargo at A shed on the north quay of the Export Dock. Also seen is No 11 Shed fruit discharging berth on the south quay of the Import Dock. Top Right: The crane is being towed by tugs from the Export Dock to the South West India Dock. The carriage is finally being loaded onto the Harrison Line M/S Explorer berthed at the mechanised H shed on the north quay of the South West India Dock.

Canary Wharf, 26 April 1957

Bottom Right: A lorry, which rolled forward from Canary Wharf into the West India Import Dock, being hoisted from the water by a dockside crane. It was being loaded with tomatoes from the Norwegian ship Bruno when the accident occurred. The driver and his mate jumped clear. The second picture shows cases of tomatoes being retrieved from the water.

London Dockers and Their Unions

Dock work was one of the hardest and tiresome trades of a hard and poor age in east London. Its worst feature was the system of casual labour. The 19th century dock companies employed a small nucleus of regular workers but the great majority were employed casually, recruited at the gates of the docks along the pavements and paid off again later the same day to suit requirements. The employers claimed that no alternative system was possible, because the amount of work they were able to offer varied considerably from day to day, depending on the number of ships in the port. High unemployment and the absence of any kind of welfare safety net such as exists today, meant there was no shortage of hands clustered on call stands at every dock gate and outside every wharf. They were desperate for a couple of hours work and the payment of a few pence, the rule was "work or starve". On some calls metal tallys carried by dockers and tally clerks, were thrown amongst the men for them to fight for with the winners getting the work.

The first major strike of dock labour against the appalling conditions came in 1888. On the 8th August a dispute flared in the South West India Dock and spread rapidly throughout the Port of London. The newly formed union, led by Ben Tillett, took control of the situation. The port was paralysed for over five weeks as the dockers pressed for their wages to be raised to 6 pence "a tanner" an hour, 2½p in modern coinage. Dockers mates became the symbol of the strike. They were backed by the public and won their demand. £13,000 was subscribed by the general public in England alone excluding alms from Trade Unions. Further sums came from the Continent and America; Australian dockers made substantial contributions. The strike ended in victory for the dockers and they won their "tanner".

By 1911 the dockers unions had been driven on to the defensive and their bargaining power

Left: (a) Veterans of the National Trade Unions meet at the Union Club in Oxford Street, London on 17th December 1930. Rt. Hon. George Lansbury, Mr James Sexton, Mr John Hodepe, Mr C W Bowlerman and Mr Ben Tillett among others joined in the music and merriment. Tom Mann emphasising a point over Sexton's head! (b) Labour leaders, Mr Ben Tillett and Mary Quail leaving No. 10 Downing Street after conciliatory conference with the Prime Minister, 12th May 1926.

Right: (a) London dockers voting to accept a substantial pay increase at the Royal Albert Dock, April 1975. Jack Dash, the Union Leader, is at the microphone. (b) London dockers held a mass meeting in Victoria Park, East London, on 22 June 1948. Mr Deakin, General Secretary of the Transport and General Workers Union, and Mr Barrett, of the Amalgamated Stevedores' Union, were invited to attend. This meeting was held at about the same time as the one at the Royal Albert Hall, nine miles away, arranged by the Union. A deputation of strikers asked Mr Deakin to cancel the Albert Hall meeting, but he refused because he would not deal with an unofficial body.

*Top: (a) **Royal Victoria Dock January 1965**, exports await loading after the inactivity at the dock when dockers continued their ban on weekend working. Ships remained idle and among the unhandled cargoes lying on the deserted quayside were cars for the Australian market. Out of 25,000 labour force, only 350 men volunteered for work - 230 at West India Docks and 120 at Surrey Docks.*
*(b) A bustling scene at **King George V Dock** early 1960s. (c) Over 80 tons of scenery and 'props' are being loaded at the King George V Dock bound for New York in August 1957, for the Sadlers Wells Opera Company. The Royal Ballet were to tour the United States.*
*Bottom: (d) **Canary Wharf, May 1962**, dockers at the West India Docks enjoy a tea break. (e) At **the Royal Victoria Docks, 1960s**, one man points out the pole from which a light will be hung for nightwork: "That's how up-to-date the docks are."*

cut down by the Shipping Federation. It was reported that their ships, the Ella, Paris and Lady Jocelyn were like troop ships ferrying hundreds of casual workers from port to port to take strikers' places. The union under the same leadership struck back and won again. Another strike took place in 1912 but the dockers were defeated and forced to surrender.

In 1920 in an attempt to prevent a national dock strike the Government appointed a judge, Lord Shaw, to lead an enquiry into the dispute. Because of his excellent presentation of the union's evidence Ernest Bevin became known as the dockers' KC (King's Counsel).

After the First World War the dockers acquired a new leader, Ernest Bevin, who became Minister of Labour in the Coalition Government during the Second World War and later held the post of Foreign Secretary in the post-war Labour Government. The General Strike of 1926 was one of the biggest ever seen in this country. It lasted nine days from 3 May and there was a big confrontation between the unions and the Government. Thousands of non-dockers were employed under armed troops and armoured vehicles to break through the picket lines.

The general public only heard of strikes when they became long lasting, but quite frequently there was a withdrawal of labour for many different reasons. The men stopped work not only for extra money but because they needed protective clothing. It was hard to get the dockers to strike because when they did they knew they would go without wages. They were reluctant men because they had responsibilities, rents to pay and kids to feed. When a dispute took place the union representatives and management met to try and resolve the problem while the men continued to do the job on a piecework basis.

After World War II the dockers' leaders were determined to end casual labour. Despite the setting up of the National Dock Labour Board casual labour in fact lasted until the 60s. By 1967 practically every docker had a regular job. Unfortunately the upper docks started to close and most of the shipping companies agreed to move down river to Tilbury Dock. Shortly after this the docks started to close one by one. Once the docks were closed all jobs were wiped out. Work was transferred away from the riverside and only about 3,000 dockers remained employed at Tilbury.

The size of the labour force was therefore reduced considerably. Lead by Jack Jones the union negotiated a severance agreement with the employers which included a lump sum payment to any men leaving the industry voluntarily, thus avoiding the need for compulsory redundancy.

Docklands Anecdotes, Museum and Stories

The stories told here are about the real East Ender dockers and the book holds nothing back in telling the truth about this remarkable and vanished breed of Londoners.

Mr Gotobed

Pilfering is a great temptation wherever you are and it did go on in Docklands. Some people were caught and ended up in court, where they were fined and then lost their jobs. Police were always on the gates and it was not easy to take anything out. If a docker had bought some books or toys for instance, and he wanted to take them out after work, he told the policeman at the gate that he had put them in the book when he went in and the entry would be scratched off. A docker asked another to buy a raincoat which was quite good and had a removable lining. It was brought in and signed for at the gate under the name of Mr Gotobed. The docker bought this coat and when he had finished work for the day he went to go out the dock gate, and the policemen said "what have you got there" and he replied a raincoat which was signed in by Mr Gotobed, "Oh" said the policeman, "and I suppose your name is Goodnight is it"? He couldn't find it in the book, so the docker said to let him have a look as it was a different policeman on duty when it was signed in, and was a horrible scrawl. But it was there and the docker did get home all right.

"Fed up to the Back Teeth"

The worst period of labour unrest during the post-war era in the UK was especially frustrating. One cartoon among many that appeared on the subject, showed a drooping, miserable man standing on a beach, looking glumly out to sea. Behind him sat his wife with two children making sand castles. A woman friend is leaning over the wife whispering; "What's the matter with Alf? Is'e sick or somefing?" "Oh no" answers the wife, "E's fed right up to the back teeth! You see e's on 'oliday and 'e could have been on strike!"

"Sugar" Marauders

At the London and St. Katharine Docks, just after the first world war, goods were taken into and out of the docks by horse and cart. On the roads leading away from the docks, poorly-clothed, bare-footed young children of both sexes would be busy under moving carts, holding paper bags under slits they had made in sacks of sugar. The children would scamper away if the cart man stopped his horses and jumped down with whip in hand, but he could not count on being free from marauders until he had driven right out of the area!

The 'Bent' Tally Clerk

Anything bulky could not be carried out of the docks. When meat was delivered for example tally clerks checked on the vans and if a bent docker knew a bent tally clerk they would collaborate. They would know a particular van driver was "alright" and give him a few hundred extra and he would give them a few quid. So the docker saw the carcasses go on, and the tally clerk checked them and made out his order. He had 400 carcasses on but in actual fact there was 500, the driver signed the receipt for 400 and could sell the extra carcasses himself as he had already paid off the docker and tally clerk. The explanation for the missing carcasses was that the ship was short loaded, as nobody could disprove it. Many bills of lading showed a container or cargo, and on the bill of lading it would have STC 100 pieces,(STC meant "said to contain") and it was only their word against the dockers.

Chinese Coins

The P & O Shipping Line carried gold bullion from China and other metals wired up and sealed, and sometimes silver coins. There would be an accident when landing, and a box dropped and the coins would run out and be quickly picked up, and so for about a week, after that, all the cigarette machines in East Ham contained nothing else but Chinese coins.

Gold Bullion

On this P & O ship which carried passengers as well as cargo, there was some precious metal sent out and there were men down the ships hold watching the bullion with police and watchmen on the quay. The bullion was loaded up out and down on the quay. On the van they were short, and they could not find out how it had gone astray. On the decks fixed to the handrail was a little wooden box with sand in it for people who were smoking and that was where the missing bullion was and nobody saw it.

"Drunken" Pig

Dockers were unloading some pork, whole pigs which had been gutted and frozen from China, huge things. A couple of dockers who were drunk wanted to get some of these pigs out, so they got an old coat, and put a hat on it, went up to the gate, and when the policeman said "whats all this", they replied "one of our mates is a bit drunk". Nobody knew the end of this story.

Hoover Iron

Pre-war people were hard up but happy. One chap got married again, but didn't get on very well with his second wife. Dockers were in the shed one day working, when all of a sudden screaming and yelling broke out. When they looked up this woman was chasing her husband round the shed with a hoover iron!

Performing Elephant

Wild animals were discharged in the docks from ships. An elephant that had been over here was going back to its country of origin and had to go on this P & O ship after everything else had been loaded. The dockers tried to lead him on to the ship, up the gangway but he just wouldn't go on, until a superintendent had a brain wave, he said "look, take the ship through the locks ready to go out, then take the elephant up there. Get the ship in the lock, lower the water so the ship drops down and the gangway becomes level for the elephant to walk on". So this is what they did.

"Healing" Air Currents

For those living in Grundy Street and Black Wall Park, the Pier and the Blackwall Tunnel were their playground; they would walk through the Tunnel to Black Heath, or catch a bus or walk to Cubitt Town, and then go via the subway to Greenwich. It was said that where the clock was and where the meridian passed there were seven different currents of air which was supposed to have healing qualities so if they were not very well that is where people were taken!

Fire Wood

In the days of coal fires, when fuel was hard to get, even after the war, dockers used to chop wood up and take a bundle out. Every now and then would be a designated hospital day, so when they got to the gate with their bundle of wood, the policeman would keep the pile of wood which was supposed to be for the hospital, but no-one knew whether the hospital actually got it. The wood was from damaged crates which were always plentiful.

Opera Props

An opera company was returning from the States, and some dockers were unloading the ship with all the scenery when they heard a bell ringing. They looked along the quay and saw a gang wearing black smocks carrying a coffin, one docker was walking in front ringing a bell. These were all opera props.

A Waxer

At London Docks, down in the wine vaults, near the Pennington Road gate, the men had a Waxer first thing every morning. Vaults were under most of the warehouses and dockers used to go down there for their Waxer - this was a drink of their choice, rum, brandy, etc.

Howes Wharf

Timber was very expensive and in Howes Wharf if the men wanted some for themselves, when the barges came up stacked 4-5ft high with timber from Surrey Docks, the lighterman would speak with another lighterman and as the barge was passed Howes Wharf some timber would accidentally fall into the water, and the tide was such that it went round and round in the river and ended up on the shore and the lads would nip down and rope it up and bring it ashore.

Durand Wharf

There used to be watermen outside the Surrey Commercial Docks in rowing boats in Greenland entrance. Quite often whilst undocking timber would be accidentally knocked over side and these waterman would put it in their rowing boats, or watermen's skips and take it to condemned hold upriver about 6 wharves up from the Greenland entrance near Durand Wharf where they would be paid for the timber classed as salvage.

Coal Jetties

Also another way of making a living was at the various coal jetties when they unloaded coal with big grabs, at Beckton, North Woolwich, & Deptford at the power station. Near Cherry Garden pier there was another power station and as the coal was unloaded via a crane some of it would drop into the water and after the ship had gone the watermen would row out and salvage the coal to sell.

Wine to Pimlico Wharf

Of the 13,000 watermen and lightermen on the Thames there were some known to be light-fingered. Sometimes the men would be ordered to Brentwood to take an empty cement barge to the Tunnel Cement Works at Purfleet and on the way would call round at Mortlake Brewery for the Watneys Barge carrying barrels of beer to Pimlico Wharf, and the men who towed the barges had all their gear ready to start tapping the barrels. They would bore a hole in them and start filling half a dozen buckets of beer, then they would tap in the fids again to seal the hole and black them over as if nothing had been touched. They would then carry on to deliver the barge. At Pimlico Wharf each worker was allowed six pints of beer per day.

Chambers Wharf

The other side of Howes Wharf was Chambers Wharf, which was a very big wharf handling the Dutch and German ships. There was also cold storage here for the handling of beef and lamb from Australia, again transferred to smaller craft to bring them up river. Looking out from the crane box towards Tower Bridge maybe 5 or 6 big ships could be seen waiting to go under the bridge to go to Butler and Hayes Wharves. One of the biggest was the Spanish line carrying mostly tomatoes and fruit. One of the ships which gave some problems was the Polish line, The Jarcon Debrovski which carried pork. Also, people coming from Communist countries would hide in the hold and many a time there was trouble when the dockers found them hiding and tried to smuggle them ashore while the crew tried to keep them on board.

Shipping Scenes 1960s

Left:(a) A tug towing barges at the eastern entrance of West India Docks. (b) Port of London Authority (PLA) warehouses at Cutler Street in the City, now demolished.

(c) Wool warehouse and wine gauging ground at London Docks and (d) Exports for shipment at the West India Docks.

Right: (e) Barges at the London Docks. (f) One of the PLA diesel-electric locomotives equipped with radio-telephone to facilitate movement control in the Royal Docks and (g) Dock gate check by PLA police constable.

Museum of Docklands

Following the closure of the docks in late 60s and early 70s the area was littered with tangible evidence of its past including river craft, dock machinery and warehousing, since the time of Dickens and in many cases since that of Chaucer. The material was lying around waiting to be scrapped. Cranes, hand carts, and many other items were to be found. There was also an enormous archive of material including photographs with details of everything from the construction of the docks to the cost of individual lock gates. It is considered that this collection is better than anywhere else in the world.

Formally handed over to the Museum of London by the Port of London Authority in 1981, the Docklands Museum was lodged in the W Warehouse, c1883, on the north side of the Royal Victoria Docks. The listed building was formerly the tobacco warehouse of the East India Dock Company. It is a huge building containing locomotives, dock crafts, over fifty in all, including rigging, cooperage, whaling and ship repairing, all displayed as though still in use. As late as the 1960s London's dockers were still using spoon-shaped shovels to move the sugar bags, making barrels and corking wine bottles by hand, using hand barrows and beam scales of a design which went back at least to the early 18th century, and carrying sugar from the West Indies on their backs down "blood alley". This was so called because the escaping grains rubbed the porters shoulders raw. The museum photographic archive backs the exhibits with contemporary images of life and work in progress including thousands of photographs. The museum is being located in the historic Grade I Listed building of No.1 Sugar Warehouse on the North Quay of the Isle of Dogs which is part of a development known as Port East, facing the Canary Wharf complex

Old Docklands. *Top Left: The industrial collections of the Museum of Docklands cover over fifty trades, including spinning, iron casting and watc making. Right: A variety of materials and tools used by the dockers are among the collections on show at the museum. Middle: Hays Wharf (now Hay Galleria), Royal Victoria and Albert Docks, early 1960s, and North Quay of Albert Dock. Bottom: Plan of Port of London 1955. It was the greatest por in the World.*

New Docklands. *Dramatic regeneration, renaissance and conservation. Top left: Luxury living and warehouse conversions at Free Trade Wharf, Wapping and Butlers Wharf, Bermondsey. Right: Development of shopping and leisure facilities at Hays Galleria, London Bridge City, Tobacco Dock and St Katharine Haven, near Tower Bridge. Middle: Life and work at Canary Wharf with transport connections to the City and Europe. Bottom: Map of today's Docklands, 1994, the most successful regeneration in the World.*

World War II Fire Fighters
Soon after the outbreak of war London's docks became an important target for the German Luftwaffe. For many consecutive nights, incendiary bombs were dropped on the West India docks and their warehouses so many, that the numerous firefighting teams were often completely unable to cope. After a number of the big warehouses had been completely destroyed by the combined action of high explosive bombs and incendiaries, an alert foreman came up with the idea of covering the top wooden floors of as many as possible of those remaining with bricks prised out of the usually still smouldering piles of rubble. This proved to be a long and difficult task, but one well worthwhile, for when it was completed, most incendiaries, after burning their way through the roofs then burnt themselves out on the bricks. It certainly saved from destruction at least two warehouses on the north quay and the goods stored in them.

Indian Seamen
As the tea boy for the gang went out of the dock and along the road outside, he may well have run across a little party of Lascars, as the Indian seamen were called. These fellows would invariably be walking along at a sedate pace in single file and one of them may well be carrying a battered second-hand sewing machine, while another may be pushing an equally decrepit bicycle, for these objects were highly prized in their homeland and were sold to supplement the man's pay-off money. The local children said that the custom of walking in single file arose from the fact that at home the Indians had to walk in single lines along the narrow jungle paths, but it was unlikely that any of the members of these ships' crews ever followed such a path.

The Whistling Pumping Station
The old pumping works, in the Royal Docks, which supplied hydraulic power to operate the lock gates, swing bridges, cranes and hoists in the docks, had an important function as far as the locals were concerned, for it was equipped with an extremely powerful steam whistle. This sounded every working morning for a full five minutes between 7.25 a.m. and 7.30 a.m. Of course, all the local factories were so equipped and their whistles sounded at various times between 7.00 a.m. and 8.00 a.m. but most of them just emitted a brief call. This was to make sure no one missed its message! People set their clocks by it.

Big Freight Containers
Post war the use of forklift trucks and pallets has developed in industry all over the world; palletised loads were becoming an increasing proportion of ships' cargoes. Suddenly however, another project appeared the employment of big freight containers in purpose built container ships. At that time, large containers were not often seen in ships' holds, as the following story may illustrate. A newly arrived ship was waiting to be discharged. The ganger (foreman) at one hold had been allocated (to his very obvious disgust) two men he had never seen before, to replace two absent regulars. He was annoyed because he believed that the 'strangers' would be inexperienced and would therefore reduce the gang's piecework earnings. Studying the cargo plan of his hold he saw that the first goods to be discharged were hundreds of small cases of canned pineapples, so he sent the 'strangers' to the gear store to collect the appropriate landing boards. The two men returned with the gear, mounted the gangway and reached the hold just as the hatches were being removed, to reveal not a multitude of small cases, but, occupying the whole area in view, two large furniture vans. After studying them and glancing back at the landing boards, one of the 'strangers' exclaimed, "Coo, they're big ain't they", "Yus mate" answered the ganger disdainfully," that's on account of their size!"

Discharging Elephants
Although the Ben Line were better known in regard to discharging at the West India Docks, a 1937 sailing card shows they loaded regularly at the docks pre Second World War. Cargoes to the West India Docks were also varied. There was a funny side to the elephants which arrived on one of their vessels the *"Benarmin"* As usual they had to be discharged on a Sunday. When they were ready no transport could be found; this was strange as the dockers had been assured the lorries would be on time. Checking round they eventually went to the police at the dock gate to see if they knew anything. Sure enough lorries had arrived about 4am in the morning, the policeman asked what they wanted and when told they were to collect elephants the drivers were chased away. No the police did not pay for the lost time!

Funny Coopers
The coopers were great characters. One man had a great trick, turning his eyelids inside out. He also wore a cloth cap, popular with many of the men, he would make it run like a wheel; up his right arm, over his head and down his left arm; all this with his eyelids turned out, he was about the funniest thing you ever saw in your life, and of course he always had everybody in fits of laughter.

Staggered Lunch Hours
The stevedores went for lunch from 12 to 1pm and the ship workers operating from the dry dock went from 1 to 2pm. Some would go along into the hold of a ship searching for ripe bananas. Somebody would suddenly shout "Tranchlas" and the ship workers ran like hell.

Banana Boats
Pre 1940 the banana boats running to the West India Docks were owned by the Banana Producers Association. They were oil burning ships compared to most other pre-war coal burners. Fuel was a major item - the pitch of the propellers was altered to save fuel. Consequently they lost time and the ship took longer to come home. Sometimes when they got to the dock the bananas had ripened and they were off loaded into barges to be taken down river to be dumped. On the way through the lock entrance, when it was high water the barges did not drop into the lock to undock and stayed level. In those days when the bridge was swung the pedestrians could cross the lock gates. If kids were passing and saw the barges, they would ask the lightermen if they could have some bananas. They would take some and tell their mates; a swarm of kids would come back and stagger away under the weight of the bananas. The Lightermen would laugh their heads off.

The Drunken Shipwrights
If a block had to be removed under a ship in a dry dock, a capping piece of timber had to be cut out. The shipwrights used long chisels and double handed mall (hammer). On one particular Saturday, having been paid on Friday, they went for a liquid lunch. On return and re-commencing work their aiming was slightly impaired and a continuous stream of shipwrights were coming out of the dry dock with black eyes and bits of blood running everywhere looking for a first aid man!

Blackwall Yard "Buggy Funnels"
On arrival in the dry dock, at 8 am in the morning and walking through the yard, all that could be seen were "Buggy Funnels" packing up from cribs (huts, home made effort) all belching smoke and no body was allowed to use these huts apart from the resident workers who included rivetters, shipwrights, (workers letting ships into the dry dock) and drillers.

The Flour Men
Dockers would be working in a flour barge all day to deliver it to another craft. The flour would be taken out of the warehouse on trucks and put at the side of the barge. Two men would pick the bag up, and hand it over the gunnel of the barge to two men down below, who would place it on their shoulders and stow it in the barge. While doing this they would wear a cloth round their head and shoulders to cover themselves and at the end of a working day, their caps and clothes would be saturated with flour. The flour would soak through as they perspired and they would end up with dough around their necks.

Rotten Hares to Antwerp
All the Steam Navigation Company ships, which operated from Irongate Wharf next to Tower Bridge, were named after birds. On one occasion a cargo of frozen hares for the Cormorant were all dumped on the quay and then the dockers went on strike and this lot was left overnight. The first mate went along with a thermometer and stuck it into these hares, over the weekend, when they were no longer frozen. So when it came for loading, the stevedores would say "oh that's all right there is nothing wrong with it." Nevertheless, the first mate would say that they remained in the rain on the dockside over the weekend and therefore were not the responsibility of the ship. Well of course, when all of this was signed it was quite a large consignment there was uproar and they went up to the head office and saw all sorts of people. When the ship got to Antwerp, people came on board with great long faces because all the hares were rotten.

Rebirth and Urban Renewal of Docklands

Regeneration of St Katharine Docks
The first urban renewal scheme started at St Katharines Docks soon after its closure. In 1969 the Greater London Council (GLC) invited proposals for the redevelopment of St Katharine Docks which would allow for the retention of the historic warehouses and the docks themselves but also provide housing, other amenities and offices. St Katharine by the Tower Limited was first formed by Taylor Woodrow to develop skills in urban renewal by directly tackling the redevelopment of the St Katharine Docks. The company submitted a scheme which envisaged the creation of a British export centre linked to a major hotel (Tower Thistle) with a conference hall and many other facilities including a yacht club. It transformed the 30 acres of derelict and war ravaged docks into a thriving business, leisure and residential community.

Redevelopment of London Docks
From the St Katharine Docks further developments took place in the London Docks at Wapping. The London Borough of Tower Hamlets showed that the revitalisation of derelict land could take place without the formation of urban development corporations. The docks were all filled in apart from Shadwell, but the experience showed the pitfalls and indeed planning restraint which would be imposed by statutory bodies which in the case of Wapping resulted in developments restricted primarily to public housing with limits of 2/3-storeys in height, out of keeping with many remaining buildings which are 5/6-storeys. It also demonstrated the inability of local councils to attract private funding to unfashionable sites, even though they were very close to the City. The warehouses on the north side of the western docks were demolished to make way for the News International Headquarters. Today the visitor will see developments throughout Wapping from Thomas Moore Street in the west to Shadwell in the east. Many of the riverside warehouses have been upgraded; some as luxury penthouse flats, some as workshops and studios. Arguably the jewel in the development of Wapping is the refurbishment of the Tobacco Dock Warehouse adjacent to Wapping Lane. The photographs here show the interior and exterior of some of these converted warehouses.

Conservation of Historic Warehouses
A survey carried out by the Department of the Environment culminated in 1983 with the listing of many 19th century warehouses as buildings of architectural or historic importance. This provided an exciting form of renovation project bringing large numbers of people to Docklands and stimulating a powerful symbol for regeneration.

An early scheme in the 1970s was Olivers Wharf, No.27, in Wapping. It was built following the Customs Consolidation Act of 1853 allowing the use as bonded stores. Once the principle of conversion was piorneered by certain developers, other companies began to look for similar opportunities. This process continued well into the 1980s resulting in many refurbishments including St Johns Wharf, No 28, in Wapping, New Concordia Wharf and Vogan Mill at St Saviours Dock, and Anchor Brewhouse and Butlers Wharf at Shad Thames. An imppresive redevelopment was the London Bridge City on the south bank. These buildings have been reborn and preserved as part of Docklands great heritage.

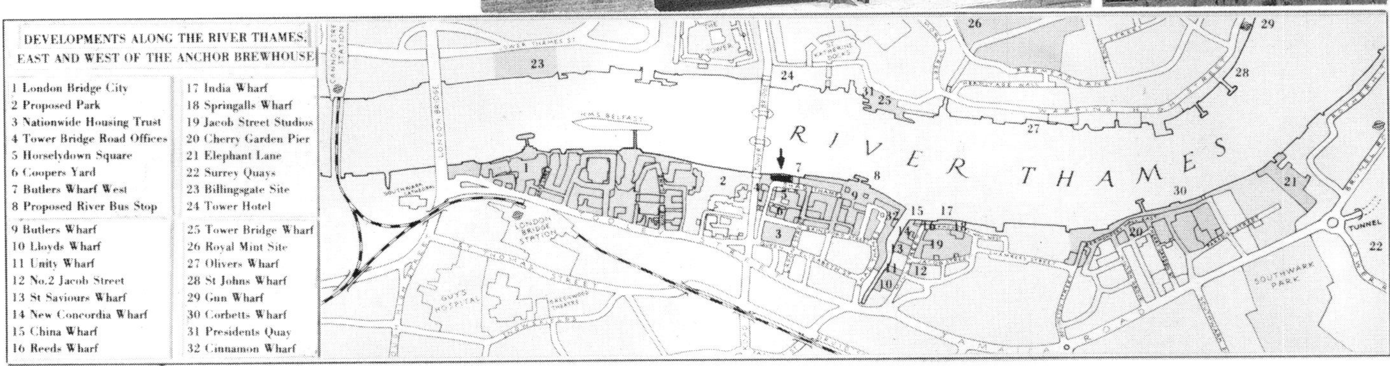

PANORAMA OF WESTMINSTER AND RIVER THAMES. *The aerial photograph shows Westminster Abbey, Houses of Parliament and Big Ben Clock Tower and County Hall, Shell Centre and Royal Festival Hall on the south bank. Westminster Pier is closeby to start your river trip.*

VIEW OF SOUTHWARK AND SOUTH BANK. *St Saviours Dock and Shad Thames are on the south side of Tower Bridge and includes New Concordia Wharf, Butlers Wharf and Anchor Brewhouse. The white building is the Design Museum. Further upstream is London Bridge City, Hays Galleria and HMS Belfast.*

THE THAMES – FROM WESTMINSTER TO CANARY WHARF

The Thames is coming full circle. Its banks are returning to their former glory. Disused buildings are being refurbished to provide offices, shops, restaurants and apartments. More and more Londoners are taking to the water, ensuring that the Riverbus service is going "full steam ahead" busily ferrying people to and from work daily.

Whether for business or pleasure, a trip down the Thames is a delight. London is shown at its best, as historic and modern landmarks slip by. From "The Houses of Parliament" to "The House they left behind", each building stands grand and important, a part of the many architectural, historical and cultural treasures flanking the river.

The Thames adds to the splendour of the City with its boats, bridges and waterside spaces. It is, however, a working river with materials and residue still being carried in and out of the City on barges.

The skyline is changing all the time. The Thames of London can be identified by great towers from Big Ben in the West to the new Tower at Canary Wharf in the East – the tallest building in the United Kingdom, another piece of London's history in the making.

N1 HOUSES OF PARLIAMENT
The Houses of Parliament are the seat of British central Government, including both the House of Commons and the House of Lords. Sir Charles Barry was commissioned to build the Houses of Parliament, in their imposing Gothic style, by Queen Victoria when the old Palace of Westminster was destroyed by fire in 1834.

N2 WHITEHALL COURT MANSIONS
Built in 1884 in the French Renaissance style and designed by Messrs Archer and Green. The Farmers Club is at No 3. The Royal Horse Guards Hotel is at No. 2.

N3 EMBANKMENT PLACE
An office and retail development above Charing Cross Station. 454,000 gross sq ft developed by Greycoat Group Plc and British Rail Property Board, designed by Terry Farrell & Company.

N4 SHELL-MEX HOUSE
500,000 sq ft of office space occupied by 2,000 members of Shell (UK's) staff.

N5 SAVOY HOTEL
The hotel was designed by T. E. Collcutt and opened in 1889 with an additional block completed in 1903-4. The Grill Room remains one of the finest hotel restaurants in London and the forecourt is the only street in the British Isles where traffic must keep to the right.

N6 SOMERSET HOUSE
Site of the first Renaissance Palace in England built in 1547-50 for Lord Protector Somerset. The house was demolished in 1775 and Sir William Chambers, The Surveyor General, was appointed architect and designed this imposing building, allocated for Government offices.

N7 TEMPLE
This is the Barristers Inns of Court which comprises the Middle Temple and the Inner Temple. The Inns of Court are formally referred to as an "Honourable Society".

N8 UNILEVER HOUSE
Unilever House, overlooking Blackfriars Bri the 300,000 sq. ft. headquarters for 1,200 U staff. The building's imposing facade was ren in 1983 and the interior is designed in an Art style.

N9 ST PAUL'S
Designed by Sir Christopher Wren and com in about 1708. Home to the Dean & Chapter Paul's.

N10 CITY OF LONDON SCHOOL
The original 'City of London School' was ope 1837 in Milk Street, off Cheapside, but move present site to facilitate its rapid growth.

N11 INTERNATIONAL TELEPHONE EXCHANGE
Built on the site of All Hallows the Great Chu Upper Thames Street, this building was com in 1976. British Telecom had the bu refurbished in 1986 and now much of the national telecommunications traffic is handled

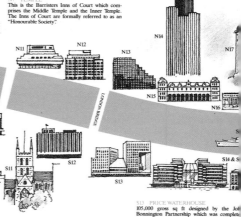

S1 ST THOMAS'S HOSPITAL
Founded in about 1106, the medical school was opened in 1871. The Board of Governors was dismissed by Act of Parliament in 1974 after four and a half centuries. The South-East Thames Regional Health Authority is now the hospital's administrative body.

S2 COUNTY HALL
Designed by Ralph Knott, work on the County Hall began in 1909, ceased in 1916 due to the war, but was resumed in 1919. The building was opened by King George V on 17 July 1922 and housed the Greater London Council until this body was dissolved in 1986.

S3 SHELL CENTRE
The headquarters of Shell International are located here. 3,500 members of staff occupying 1,100,000 sq ft.

S4 ROYAL FESTIVAL HALL
A large concert hall and arts complex which was designed by Sir Robert Matthew and Sir J L Martin (1945-1951) and Sir Hubert Bennett (1962-1965). It was opened in 1951 as a celebration of the Festival of Britain. Festival Pier also accommodates a riverbus station which is a convenient eight minutes walk from Waterloo Station.

S5 LONDON WEEKEND TELEVISION
Completed in 1971, this building houses LWT's television studios. The tower is occupied partly by LWT but also leased to others including P&O Bulk Shipping.

S6 SEA CONTAINERS HOUSE
Designed by the Fitzroy Robinson Partnership and completed in 1986, Sea Containers House is a reconstruction of a 1970s building originally designed as an hotel. Main letting to HM Customs & Excise.

S7 DAILY EXPRESS
Developed by The Fleet Street Partnership and designed by the Fitzroy Robinson Partnership, this building is 525,000 gross sq ft with 11 storeys.

S8 BANKSIDE POWER STATION
Bankside Power Station was designed by Sir Giles Scott and opened in 1963. It occupies the site of the Great Pike Gardens in Southwark.

S9 GLOBE THEATRE
This site (owned by Hanson Plc) was originally to be developed into office buildings until part of the remains of Shakespeare's old Globe Theatre were discovered there. The new Globe Theatre will now be built on this area as well as the planned office space.

S10 FINANCIAL TIMES
With a gross square footage of 212,000 square feet, this building was completed in 1988 and is home to the Financial Times editorial and advertising staff as well as Cable News Network. It was designed by the T P Bennett Partnership.

S11 SOUTHWARK CATHEDRAL
This is the earliest Gothic church in London, dating from 1220. It is the 4th church to have been built on this site, the three earlier ones having been destroyed by fire. The Cathedral is rich in monuments such as the memorial to Shakespeare carved in 1912 by Henry McCarthy. A birthday service for Shakespeare is held here every year.

S12 GLAZIERS HALL
The earliest record of the Glaziers is in 1328 and the Hall was first mentioned in 1601 when it was situated in Five Foot Lane, off Queen Victoria Street. This was lost in the Great Fire and not rebuilt. The present day Glaziers Hall was designed by William Holford and opened in 1978. It is shared with the Scientific Instrument Makers and includes many commercial offices.

S13 PRICE WATERHOUSE
105,000 gross sq ft designed by the Jo Bonnington Partnership which was complet 1986. Developed by St Martin's Pro Corporation Limited.

S14 & S15 HAY'S GALLERIA
Formerly Hay's Dock, this site now has 35 gross sq ft of office space, retail and leisure fac designed by Michael Twigg Brown & Partner developed by St Martin's Property Corpor Ltd. Lloyds Bank occupy 160,000 sq ft wit remaining space let in small units.

S16 HMS BELFAST
At 11,000 tons, HMS Belfast was the largest cr ever built for the Royal Navy. She was built in and first opened to the public in 1971.

S17 BUTLER'S WHARF
Warehouses dating from 1870's, now developed as a major complex of offices, studios, workshops, leisure units, a sports c and a shopping area.

VIEW OF ST KATHARINE AND THE CITY. *On the north side of the river are the new developments of Tower Bridge Wharf, President Quay, the headquarters of the Royal Naval Reserve, and Tower Thistle Hotel. The Tower of London, Custom House, St Paul's Cathedral and the City of London are at the top right corner.*

THE PROSPECTS OF LONDON DOCKLANDS FROM GREENWICH. *The picture, looking north, shows the extensive and dramatic re-development of the Isle of Dogs and its transformation into a world-class financial centre. The offices on Canary Wharf are spread around a boulevard and a series of traditional London squares with green open spaces.*

ARCLAYS DE ZOETE
ed in 1984, Barclays de Zoete and Barclays at Bank occupied the 129,000-sq ft in 1985. lding was designed by Whinney Mackay-c.

IDLAND MONTAGU
sq ft with glass exterior designed by Covell vs Wheatley. Home to Midland Montagu a owned investment banking subsidiary of Bank.

ATIONAL WESTMINSTER TOWER
nembers of National Westminster's staff this elegant tower – part of the bank's ional division. The tower was designed by R Seifert and Partners and in its ction required 100,000 tonnes of concrete 0 tonnes of steel. It is 600 feet tall, 200 than the Canary Wharf Tower.

N15 OLD BILLINGSGATE FISH MARKET
A major reconstruction of the Old Billingsgate Market (following its move to the Isle of Dogs in 1982) was completed in 1989. There is 120,000 gross sq ft designed by Richard Rogers Partnership. The new Billingsgate Market is close to Port East adjacent to Canary Wharf.

N16 THE CUSTOM HOUSE
In 979 King Ethelred levied the first known customs duty. Since then the Customs House has been built and rebuilt a total of six times due to fire, gun-powder explosions and war. Major refurbishment being proposed by HM Customs & Excise.

N17 TOWER OF LONDON
The Tower of London is a splendidly preserved Medieval fortress which to date has been a palace, prison and place of execution as well as housing royal armouries. The Crown Jewels are still guarded here.

N18 TOWER THISTLE HOTEL
Built to the designs of the Renton Howard Wood Partnership in 1973, The Tower Thistle Hotel is part of the St Katharine's Dock development.

N19 ST KATHARINE'S DOCK
The Docks were designed by Thomas Telford and opened in 1828. They were closed in 1968 and sold by the Port of London Authority to the Greater London Council. Since then there has been massive redevelopment producing office, retail and residential space. The London Commodity Exchange and Reuters have office space here, among others.

N20 BOATYARD
This is the River Police boatyard used for their launch repairs. It stands on the site of the old Execution Dock. Captain Kidd is believed to be the last pirate executed here.

N21 HEADQUARTERS OF THE RIVER BOAT POLICE
This is the oldest police force in the world. Formed in the early 1720's, it dates back earlier than the Bow Street Runners.

N22 PROSPECT OF WHITBY
This is one of the oldest riverside public houses. Built in 1520, it was known as Devil's Tavern due to the clientele it attracted at that time. Its name was changed to the present one after a ship called 'Prospect' moored off the tavern and became a landmark.

N23 PROSPECT WHARF
Developed by Trafalgar House Residential and designed by Shepheard Epstein & Hunter. Prospect Wharf is wholly residential.

N24 FREE TRADE WHARF
Recently refurbished to provide new offices and housing with leisure and retail facilities. Developed by Regalian Properties plc.

N25 STEPNEY POWER STATION
This is an old disused Power Station for Stepney which is currently unoccupied.

N26 THE GRAPES
A 16th Century public house which was frequented (so it is said) by Dickens. It holds an early morning licence for dockers.

N27 CASCADES
Built in 1987 by Kentish Homes. Cascades is a residential development with its own sports facilities including swimming pool and gymnasium.

N28 THE ANCHORAGE
The Anchorage was developed by Rosehaugh Co Partnership Developments and designed by Michael Squire Associates. It is a wholly residential development.

N29 CANARY WHARF
Canary Wharf is the world's largest commercial development and will be the centre of London's third business district. The project will provide 10 million sq ft of new office space, including Britain's tallest building, measuring 800 ft. The 24 buildings are interconnected by parks, squares, courtyards and waterside promenades providing a new working environment in Docklands.

N23
N24
N25
N26
N27
N28
N29
S23
S24
S25
S26
S27
S28

S28 THE MILLENNIUM EXHIBITION SITE

S21 BRAITHWAITE & DEAN
Braithwaite & Dean is an old and established lighterage company whose offices are located in what is often referred to as "The house they left behind." The other houses which formed a terrace were destroyed by bombing during the war. This is the only one to survive and is now protected by a preservation order.

DESIGN MUSEUM
Design Museum is a reconstruction of a dant 1950's Thames-side warehouse and ed by Conran Roche. The Museum's main is to illustrate the styles and developments of entury mass produced design.

JACOBS ISLAND
a development of studios and apartments. s Island first became famous as the site of Bill s death in Oliver Twist. The present-day Jacob marks the site.

THE ANGEL
public house dates back to the mid 1700's. It is hat the Judge Jefferies took wine here while ecutions he had ordered were carried out the river at Execution Dock.

S22 PRINCESS IRON WORKS
An old and established barge yard.

S23 ST MARY'S CHURCH
Completed in 1715, St Mary's Church has strong maritime connections. The captain of the Mayflower, Christopher Jones, was buried in the churchyard in 1622.

S24 SCANDIC CROWN HOTEL
London's Docklands newest international hotel opened in April 1991. The hotel is four star rated and has one block of three converted from the 19th century Columbia Wharf.

S25 GREENLAND PASSAGE
Located by Greenland Dock and South Dock Marina, this passage got its name from the many ships which docked here before leaving for Greenland.

S26 SURREY QUAYS RETAIL CENTRE
Opened on 25th October 1988, the Surrey Quays Retail Centre provides 280,000 sq ft of shopping facilities with such names as Tesco, BHS and Boots as well as a foodcourt. The relaxed and nautical atmosphere is created by the surrounding fountains and pools.

S27 GREENWICH TOWN CENTRE
Greenwich is the place from where the world's time is measured and is also hosting the National millennium.

Building of a New City in Docklands 1980s

The regeneration of London Docklands and the building of a new city started early in 1980. Its unique environment covers a total area of 20 sq.km - its scale and location clearly conveying a city dimension. A number of factors had combined to leave Docklands as an area until then without stature. Historically and physically, the docks were cut off from the mainstream of London life, hidden behind high brick walls, and thus restrained from any tendency to spread westward. The area was derelict and it was presented as the worst problem area in the country with land values generally low. As a result there was almost a complete absence of new private investment. There was a total dependence on public sector funded programmes under the Local Authorities. As a result an almost complete economic void existed which had to be filled by areas of activities with future growth potential. There was widespread disbelief that anything would actually happen whichever agency was responsible.

London Docklands Development Corporation (LDDC)

Following the general election in 1979, the Conservative Party, led by Margaret Thatcher, came to power. Michael Heseltine, the then Secretary of State for the Environment, announced that he did not consider the Local Authorities had made sufficient progress in the regeneration of London Docklands and intended to appoint a new organisation to take over the task. He considered the area as a major opportunity for urban regeneration and development of London in the last two decades of the 20th century. There was a need for new housing, industrial and commercial developments, and recreational facilities. The view by Government was that the transformation from decline to renewal could only be achieved by a level of public expenditure through a single-minded development agency.

To set up the LDDC, the Secretary of State first had to persuade Parliament to pass an Act allowing the Government to establish Urban Development Corporations modelled on those for the new towns which were established during the 1940s, 50s and 60s and led to the establishment of Town Corporations such as Stevenage and Milton Keynes. The local Government Planning and Land Act of 1980 allowed the Secretary of State to designate any area of land as an Urban Development Area (UDA) and to establish an Urban Development Corporation (UDC) to generate an Urban Development Area. Because of the strong objections by the Greater London Council (GLC) and other local boroughs and petitions against the proposed LDDC, an all party select committee of the House of Lords was asked to report on the matter. The Government then had to explain to this committee why it wished to transfer the power of controlled development in Docklands from the democratically elected borough councils to a Corporation whose members are appointed by the Environment Secretary who was accountable only to Parliament. The all party select committee finally recommended that the LDDC be set up. The arguments which were put against the establishment of the corporation included that if the body was formed the power to control development would be taken away from the democratically elected borough councils to a quango appointed by Government.

As a result Parliament passed an Act in 1981 to form the London Docklands Development Corporation (LDDC) with Sir Nigel Broakes as its Chairman. Its initial objectives and priorities were very clear; in order to reverse the area's long economic, social and physical decline there had to be a radical change in the projections of its image and opportunities. Docklands was divided into four areas; Wapping and Limehouse, the Isle of Dogs, the Surrey Docks and the Royal Docks. The Isle of Dogs Enterprise Zone (EZ) was set up in 1982 as an incentive to attract investment into the area. Within its borders few planning restraints were put on the early builders. Developers and Companies moving into the area would benefit for ten years from a variety of tax and rate incentives.

Sequence of Development Events
Random Initiatives

An early decision was made to drop Greenwich and Lewisham as there was quite enough to do in the other three boroughs and not a great deal in these two. Hays Wharf was added by Micheal Heseltine to the area. There were not many staff for the LDDC at the time. The corporation came through in July 1981, when the select committe under Lord Cross reported. He declared it was a draconian measure but justified to deal with problems which were not of local or even metropolitan importance, but were of national importance.

Another early decision made was to focus on the Isle of Dogs instead of starting from the western end near Tower Bridge, and a great deal of importance was given to the formation of the Enterprise Zone. There was a strong feeling that without an Enterprise zones the development of London Docklands would have been seriously retarded. It appears that Geoffrey Howe helped in establishing the Enterprise zone on the Isle of Dogs. He was then Chancellor and very sympathetic because the Bow group which he had founded, had started in Bow and he declared the invention of an exterprise zone on site on the Isle of Dogs and the LDDC was lucky there. Wandsworth Borough Council was the other blue-eyed boy of the Conservative establishment at the time, and they put up a very good case, according to Nigel Broakes. The Isle of Dogs had a population of about 13000, Jobs had fallen from 6000 to a few hundred and there was no question at the time of attracting major offices and businesses into the area. The first glimmer of development was Limehouse Studios on Canary Wharf using one of the empty warehouses. It brought in people who wanted to live locally and were very happy to move into the east end.

New Housing Development

There is no evidence to prove that the re-development of Docklands during the first half of the 1980s was the result of a master plan. At no time was there any such plan produced for Docklands and what happened was the result of a series of apparently random and ad-hoc initiatives which later had a coherence. The first thing which the LDDC had to do was to adopt a fresh perception of the place and try to communicate with people and developers. The second was getting the marketplace to realise how near the location was to the City. In this respect the Chief Executive, Reg Ward, issued a challenge for redevelopment in May 1981. Over 90% of the housing stock was public sector, less than 5% owner occupied and only a few new houses had been built for private occupation in the previous 5-6 years. It was somewhere that nobody wanted to go and it was not perceived there was a role for private sector housing in the area. This was made an opportunity for changing the situation. If there was less than 5% owner-occupation against an overall London average of 60% there had to be a huge demand which was not being met.

Fortunately four house builders responded to the challenge and asked if they could be found a 30 acre site. They would be committed to building 600 houses over the next 3 years whether they were sold or not. By February 1982, less than seven months from the initial challenge, Michael Heseltine opened the first show houses. By that summer all the houses were pre-sold and the builders were asking for more land. They were sold another 50 acres and it was that simple arrangement which has given rise to the largest private-sector housing programme ever achieved in the UK. Around 17,000 houses were completed by 1991.

Docklands Light Railway (DLR)

At the same time as house development was vigorously pursued the concept of the light railway system was discussed. In the summer of 1980, the Secretary of State for Transport and the Chairman of the GLC, Horace Cutler, announced the demise of the Jubilee Line extension which was to have gone right through Docklands to Thamesmead. The project was to be completed in the year 2000 at a cost of £600m. The LDDC was required to regenerate the area in a short period of time and the deadline for the extension was too far away to help with this. It was observed that a large quantity of British Rail track lying all in the right place was either unused or seriously under-used and the idea of running the

Docklands Light Railway on this track was then conceived. Neither the GLC nor London Transport were particularly interested but by the time a solution was proposed in July 1981 they rallied very actively. Twelve months later the Government approved the Docklands Light Railway plan.

The moment the railway was confirmed it did four things for Docklands. Firstly, this was a major new piece of infrastructure which created value around the sites it actually served. Secondly, it was a public transport system badly needed, and thirdly, and this was significant, it provided an important showcase for people to start thinking about Docklands as a possible location where exciting things might actually happen. As a result a wide debate started to take place which was helpful in marketing the area. The fourth benefit and this was totally accidental, by linking Tower Bridge and the approach to Greenwich Tunnel Island Gardens, the Dockland Light Railway provided the first new tourist link for over forty years. So it was again a good example of actually creating an opportunity out of the project.

London City Airport (The Stolport)
Although the success of the housing development and the approval of the DLR were very encouraging there was a great deal of doubt about the redevelopment of the Royal Docks. It was thought nothing would happen until the year 2000 when a new road would be built to the eastern boundary and crossing over the river. This created a new challenge for transport development. There was a meeting between the Chairman of Mowlem's, building and civil engineering contractors, Philip Beck, and Reg Ward, to discuss the concept of stolport and Dash Seven. Shortly afterwards the Chief Executive of Brymon Airways, who had experience of Dash Seven aircraft got involved with the project. Just before Christmas 1984 Philip Beck submitted proposals for the stolport on the south side of the Royal Albert Docks. Three years and a major public enquiry later the Secretary of State approved the lift-off for the project. Only five miles from the City the new airport was thought to transform the daily travel of business people. Also in the course of investigating levels of electro-magnetic interference in the zone, which might interfere with the Dash Seven landing technology, it was discovered that because no one had any interest in the area all major telecommunication beacons bypass it. So it was in fact the last interference free zone in London in communication terms.

British Telecom
The above discovery encouraged the LDDC to start negotiations with British Telecom who decided to build a satellite earth station in North Woolwich, which became operational nine months later. Other companies such as Mercury were also persuaded to build their satellite earth station on the Isle of Dogs. This competition gave rise to perhaps the most significant infrastructure commitment of them all when at the end of 1983 British Telecom decided to put a fibre-optic ring main right through Docklands to North Woolwich when there wasn't a single end user in sight.

(a) Sir Nigel Broakes Chairing a meeting of the first London Docklands Development Corporation (LDDC) Committee with Reginald Ward, the Chief Executive, on his left c1981. (b) Environment Secretary, Michael Heseltine(left), meets the newly appointed LDDC Chief Executive, Eric Sorensen and the Chairman, David Hardy,(centre) c1991.

Canary Wharf Project
A series of happenings up to 1985 shaped the future of Docklands and perhaps produced the first framework which made Canary Wharf a possibility on the Isle of Dogs. At the time the Americans were actually looking for space in London and came looking in Docklands and here the Canary Wharf proposal was perhaps the most significant lucky coincidence of all. Few people realise that Canary Wharf rose out of a search for 5000 sq.ft building for the Roux Brothers restaurant chain. The Chairman of Credit Suisse, came to Docklands and went on an old Thames barge which happened to be moored right alongside a warehouse on Canary Wharf. Many more visits to Docklands followed by the Americans and the back-up office concept changed the consideration of an office development which resulted in the proposals by G Ware Travelsted for Canary Wharf to be submitted in 1985 at an estimated cost of £3 -£4 billion, to create the world's largest commercial development offering superb office facilities.

What did change most significantly in 1986 was the scale of development. The proposal for a major financial centre of 12 million sq.ft of Canary Wharf was both a reflection on the new perception of Docklands and a stimulus to it. At a stroke it raised the general perception of development onto a higher plane. Approval in principle by the LDDC coincided with the announcement by the Bank of England that it was no longer essential for bankers to be located within the City's square mile. With the de-regulation of the London financial market and the consequent need for increased floor space and specialised office and trading accommodation there was an opportunity for an eastward extension of London's financial centre. Due to lack of cash the originator withdrew and the scheme was taken over by the Canadian developers Olympia and York who started piling work in March 1988. By that time investment in the area began to develop and within a short period of time Docklands was recognised as a major opportunity area. Indeed most national newspapers moved in from Fleet Street. Many thousands of new jobs were created. The scale of construction was massive and Docklands became a fashionable area in which to live, work and enjoy leisure time.

CANARY WHARF

1988

- The top picture shows construction on the Isle of Dogs in January 1988.
- The inset picture of Canary Wharf when in April 1988, the developers Olympia & York moved in to start to build their giant office complex.
- Access to the far end of the wharf is gained by installing a Bailey bridge. The Westferry Circus roundabout begins to take shape.
- In April, the first sheet pile is driven for the cofferdam for the tower. The infrastructure works and piling get under way.
- The House of Commons Public Accounts Committee gives London Docklands Development Corporation a roasting over selling land to Olympia & York for only £160,000/ha.
- Marine piling has acoustic shrouds or muffers in action to deaden the noise. Massive piling cases arrive by ship, saving major road traffic headache.
- Around 1200 staff and workforce on site. Barge movements hit 300 per month.

1989

- Tower crane spotter's paradise with 36 specimens to admire.
- Work begins on the last remaining building - 25 North Colonade.
- An eight-week unofficial strike by steel erectors followed by a work-to-rule hits the project. Worst affected is the tower - the strike and other problems during steel erection limit progress to the 12-storey mark by the year's end.
- Startling progress on site in November 1989 as the developers beat the steel strike and start a second building phase - seven months ahead of schedule.
- 30 South Colonade becomes the first building to be topped-out.
- Barge movements peak at 500 per month. Staff and workforce soar to 2800 by year's end.
- Total concrete batched on site since work began exceeds 180,000 m^3.
- Merrill Lynch becomes one of the first customers to take space.
- The Canary Wharf Tower climbed steadily to 12 floors - or 200 ft - above the West India Dock and started to soar at the scheduled rate of three floors a fortnight.

SNAPSHOT PROGRESS

1990

- The first "topping out" ceremony at Canary Wharf took place in February 1990 when a 13-storey office building was completed.
- In March, Olympia & York removes Ellis-Don McAlpine on the tower - then at floor 21. Within eight months, 29-storeys are added and the tower is topped-out. All first phase buildings are topped-out.
- Upper deck of the Westferry Circus roundabout is completed. Alongside, piling rigs move in to start work on the 95,000 m2 second phase buildings - six months ahead of schedule. At the far end of the dock, piling hammers ring out as the £17m cofferdam for phase three is constructed.
- Staff and workforce hit a peak at 4,500. Up to 300 barge movements per month.

1991

- The first tenants move in to Canary Wharf in August. Olympia & York announces letting arrangements reached for 57% of the near 500,000 m^2 of the office and retail space available on the first and second phase buildings under construction.
- Since the start of the job, more than 3,200 firms have been employed on the wharf, more than 360,000 m^3 of concrete has been batched on site, more than 8,000 barge loads of materials have been delivered to the site.
- Staff and workforce start to reduce - 3000 in June and falling. Barge movements tail of to nothing by June as first phase reaches completion.
- In London, office over-capacity hits new high with more than 2 million m^2 of space unlet. Olympia & York are not saying when phase three will start but plans drawn up in 1990 indicate a 1992 lift off.

1992

- Five lasers, 14 search lights and 800 floodlights ensured that Canary Wharf gave a unique and spectacular welcome on New Year's Eve. The light show was accompanied by foghorns and fireworks.

Heritage Trails and Walks on the Isle of Dogs

North Quay and Canary Wharf

This heritage trail provides a route which passes a number of interesting, new and old, buildings and places. Although it is a fair walk round the island it is possible to cut corners by the use of the Docklands Light Railway or Docklands Bus. The best way to see the Isle of Dogs is from the elevated track of the DLR. You get magnificent views of the conservation areas, the docks and the new buildings. At the north east corner of the island is the West India Dock Conservation Area which contains the most important group of buildings built by the Dock Company. (See photographs and map on pages 46 and 47).

A convenient point to start this heritage trail is the DLR Westferry Station. Walk a short distance along Westferry Road and take the first left into Garford Street. On your right you see the **three Georgian Cottages, No 1,** with slated roofs which are the last surviving buildings of their kind and are Grade II Listed. They were built in 1819 by John Rennie, engineer for the West India Dock Company, to house the Police staff within the dock estate. The cottages have been renovated and are now private residences. At the end of this street turn right into Hertsmere Road. **The Salvation Army Building, No 2,** is on your right. It was designed by Niven and Wigglesworth in 1902. This pretty Queen Anne style building was opened by the Ambassador to Sweden and Norway and run by two Sisters as a mission to Scandinavian seamen until it was given to the Salvation Army in 1930. Further along is the **Dockmasters House, No 3,** designed by Thomas Morris, the resident engineer to the Dock Company in 1807. Originally opposite the Customs Office, it was first used as an Excise Office, then became the Jamaica Tavern, reverting under the Port of London Authority to dock use as the Dock Managers Office, and now is privately owned and has been redeveloped into a restaurant. Adjacent to this building is the old entrance to the West India Docks, the **piers, No 4,** of which date back to 1803.

Following Hertsmere Road you come across the general dock office **Ledger Building, No 5,** and the magnificent **Sugar Warehouses 1 and 2, No 6,** which were designed by George Gwilt and his son, and are the finest examples of early 19th century dock architecture surviving anywhere. The warehouses were completed in 1802 and have magnificent cast iron spiked windows on the ground floor. The Warehouses are being converted into a leisure complex called Port East, incorporating the Museum in Docklands. The circular **Guard House, No 7,** on the other side of the road, was designed by George Gwilt in 1803, originally one of a pair the building was used as an armoury and also as a temporary lock-up for thieves.. The adjacent quadrangle building, **Cannon Workshop, No 8,** was once a cooperage workshop for the Port of London Authority and now provides accommodation for a number of small businesses. The splendid entrance arch was built in 1825 by Sir John Rennie. A Trinity high water mark on the wall below the arch shows how low the land is.

Turn into Ontario Road and walk up the ramp to **Canary Wharf, No 9,** complex and start at the Westferry Circus which is beautifully landscaped with excellent views of the Thames and the Surrey Docks. Follow West India Road eastwards and you arrive in Cabot Square with its beautiful water fountain. The complex of new offices, concert hall, restaurants, pubs, shops and market stalls have become one of London's dominant landmarks. Caesar Pelli's, 246m **Tower, No 10,** is one of the great buildings of the late 20th century. The **West India Import, No 11,** and **Export Docks, No 12,** on the north and south side of Canary Wharf were opened in 1802 and 1806 respectively. In Fisherman's Walk, north side of Canary Wharf, is the new pub of **The Cat & The Canary, No 13,** which overlooks the historic Import Dock. On the south side is **The Henry Addington, No 14,** an American style bar overlooking the Export Dock.

Westferry Road and Millwall

From Canary Wharf follow along Marsh Wall and on your right you will see the **Pumping Station, No 15,** built 1909 at the entrance to the South West India Dock and two new developments of the **Cascades** and **Anchorage**. Further along on the left can be seen **Britannia International Hotel** followed by further new buildings and developments including **South Quay Plaza, No 16**. At the traffic lights turn right into Mill Harbour and proceed along **Millwall Inner Dock, No 17**, c1868, to Pepper Street. To your left is a new development of **Glengall Bridge, No 18**, which is occupied by a London Business School, part of the University in Phoenix, Arizona, USA.. From Pepper Street continue along Teller Road until you reach Westferry Road where you can turn left to proceed south. At Claude Street you reach the former **Church of St Paul's, No 19**, built in 1856 by Thomas Knightly. The church is built in coloured brick and stone. Opposite on the river side is the new development of Cyclops, No 20, along Homer Drive. Continue walking in a southerly direction and you will arrive on your left at **Harbinger Road Primary School, No 21**, which was built in 1908 and is still in use. The original name, British Street Millwall School, is set in attractive tiles on the side facing Marsh Street. The two **Terraces of Cottages, No 22**, in Harbinger Road and Cahir Street are some of the last surviving dockers' and workers' houses on the island. Opposite on the river side are the new development of **Burrells Wharf, No 23**, the site of the **Great Eastern** launch. This was the first site in the country laid out for large scale iron ship building. Its owner at the time, William Fairbairn, was also a pioneer of structural iron work and tested models of Stevenson,s Britannia Bridge Pier. The yard was later bought by John Scott Russell who built the Great Eastern between 1853-58. It was one of the engineering wonders of the World attracting many visitors to admire the paddle and screw ship as it grew parallel to the Thames on extra land rented from David Napier. The remains of one of the two 120ft long **Slipways, No 24**, was found in 1984.. Designed by Isambad Kingdom Brunel and built for the Eastern Steam Navigation Company the ship was a vast 692ft long. Adjacent to Burrell's Wharf, the **Maconochies Wharf** is the largest self-built development of houses in Britain.

Further along Westferry Road is the **Chapel House Estate, No 25**, in Chapel House Street. George Lansbury cut the first turf for these First World War homes for heroes in 1919. Named after the local Medieval Chapel which was located on the site of the nearby. Housing was built by Poplar Borough Council in 1926 and 1933. From Chapel House Street turn right into Eastferry Road and you find the **Docklands Settlement, No 26**, on your left. As "The Welcome House" this building was opened in 1905 as a club and dining room for local factory girls. It was bought by the Docklands Settlement Movement in 1923. If you walk across to **Millwall Park** you see the **Railway Viaduct, No 27**, which was built in 1872 when the railway was extended south from Millwall Dock to the terminus at North Greenwich. The structure is now used by the Docklands Light Railway.

Island Gardens

At the junction of Westferry and Eastferry Roads is the "Queen Anne" style building of the **Fire Station, No 28**, dating from 1904 and built by the London County Council. The original cottages remain behind. Crossing Manchester Road into Ferry Street you find the **Ferry House Pub, No 29**. At one time this was the only building on the southern tip of the isle apart from the Chapel House. It linked in with the ferry and passengers from south of the river would continue their journey up Eastferry Road. It is recorded that Pepys used this ferry in 1665. The Ferry House was rebuilt in the 19th century. On the riverside is the new housing development of **Luralda Wharf** and close by along Westferry Road is **The Lord Nelson Pub, No 30**, built around 1859. Walk eastwards towards **Island Gardens** and the entrance to the **Foot Tunnel to Greenwich, No 31**. The gardens were laid out by Poplar Borough Council and the London County Council in 1895 and they give excellent views across the Thames of Greenwich and the Royal Observatory and the Cutty Sark.

The **Foot Tunnel** opened in 1902, replacing the ferry, and catered mainly for dockers coming from the south and Greenwich. To the west of the gardens is **Johnsons Draw Dock**, No 32. Walking the other way eastward you

The area is steeped in naval history: Columbus and Cabot came to petition Henry VII for support for their voyages to the New World; Sir Francis Drake was knighted by Queen Elizabeth I on board his ship, the "Golden Hind"; Peter the Great of Russia learned about navigation here; Captains Cook and Bligh lived here, as well as Sir Walter Raleigh; Lord Nelson's state funeral procession sailed around the Isle of Dogs, and Cleopatra's Needle travelled the same route on its last few miles from Alexandria, Egypt, to its present location on the Embankment.

Henry VIII

THE ISLE OF DOGS

The Isle of Dogs is a peninsula, jutting south into the Thames, bounded by Limehouse, Greenwich and Blackwall Reaches.

It is believed that the origin of the name comes from the fact that Charles II kept the Royal Kennels in this marshy area, away from the Royal Palace at Greenwich.

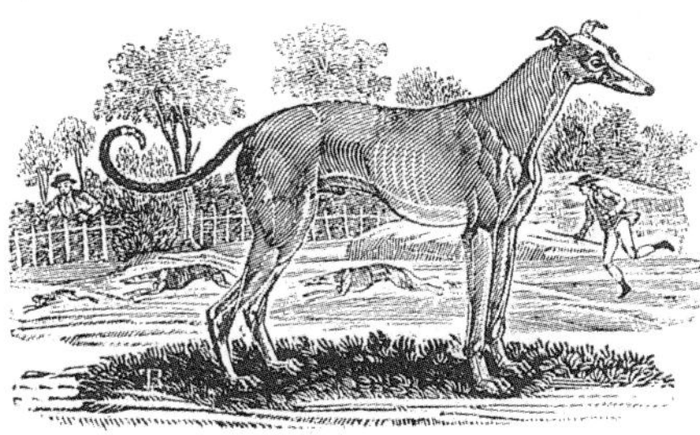

Bells have played an important part in the history of the region. Its inhabitants are known as "Cockneys," if they were born within the sound of Bow Bells.
The bell recovered from the sunken "Lutine" is traditionally rung at Lloyds of London, to announce the loss of a vessel.
The nearby bell foundry at Whitechapel, where the famous American Liberty bell was cast, is still in operation today.

The "Liberty Bell"

Sir Francis Drake

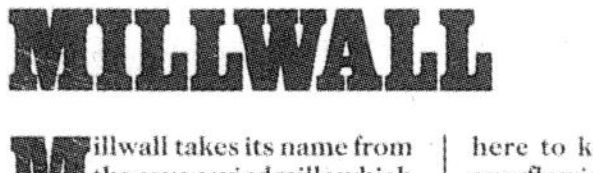

MILLWALL

Millwall takes its name from the seven windmills which stood on the wall built here to keep the Thames from overflowing at high tide.

Hanging Sign, Lombard Street

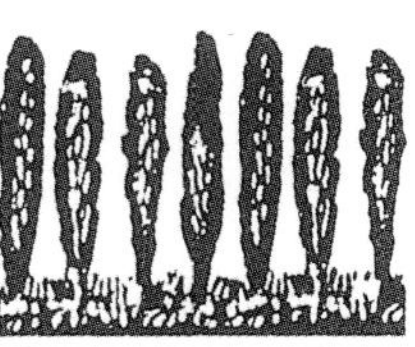

POPLAR

The borough of Poplar derives its name from the abundance of Poplar trees that once grew in this area. It is a curious connection that the Lombardy Poplar tree takes its name from the northern Italian region and family of moneylenders, who came to England in the wake of the Norman conquest—hence the name Lombard Street, the Wall Street of London!

Parish boundery mark, 1886. Canary Wharf is within the Parish Of All Saint's Poplar.

At the centre of Canary Wharf stood Rum Quay. The Quay was enclosed by an immense, 25 foot wide glass roof, which is believed to have originally formed a covered walkway into the Crystal Palace when it was first erected in Hyde Park in 1851 to house the Great Exhibition.
Inside the structure were stored enormous puncheons of rum, each holding 103 gallons of spirit. On Rum Quay, curfew bells were mounted on a 45 ft. high iron ship's mast, which traditionally were rung for ten minutes every night and morning, marking the time period when no fires or candles were permitted to be burnt on the ships. This was to protect the highly flammable rum spirit. As late as 1928 the Rum Quay bells were still in use for time-keeping purposes, being rung at midday, and again an hour later.

Trinity House high water mark

The borough of Poplar has now been absorbed into the district of Tower Hamlets.

A ship canal was cut, connecting Limehouse and Blackwall Reaches to obviate the circuitous route around the Isle of Dogs, however, it proved a failure and was later turned into a timber dock, now known as "South Dock."

come to **Newcastle Draw Dock, No 33**, which was used by small coasters and barges which would pull in at high tide for unloading into carts on the beach when it ebbed. The draw dock was built c1850. In Glenafric Avenue is **Watermens Arms, No 34**, a pub with wrought iron balconies, formerly known as the Newcastle Arms. The idea of Enterprise Zone was launched here by Sir Geoffrey Howe at a dinner in 1981. Close by is **Christchurch, No 35**, which was designed by Johnson in the early 1850s with donation by William Cubitt of £7000. William Cubitt is still remembered in Cubitt Town. He became an MP for Andover and was twice Lord Mayor of the City of London.

Mudchute, Coldharbour and Blackwall

The **Island's History Trust** is housed along Manchester Road and near Christchurch. The trust has a huge collection of several thousand local photographs and serves an excellent source of information on the Island's history. Cross Manchester Road into Seyssell Street and then turn left and right again into **Globe Road Walk, No 36**. This was formerly the site of rail tracks used by rope laying machines. From there you walk towards the **Mudchute Farm, No 37**. Walk north through the park until you reach **Asda Superstore, No 38**, along Eastferry Road. An Edwardian stone building dating from 1904 with timber cupola is the **Carnegie Public Library, No 39**, in Strattondale Street. Continue along this road passing the **London Arena** until you come to the **Docklands Visitor Centre, No 40**, on your right, opposite the new development of **Harbour Exchange**.

Continue walking north along Limeharbour at the junction and turn right into Marsh Wall and the new **Community Centre, No 41,** for the Island near the end of the road. The new **Pumping Station, No 42,** in Stewart Street is worth a visit. Turn back into Preston Road and the **Blue Bridge, No 43** becomes visible. This is a large modern Dutch style draw bridge built by the Port of London Authority in 1969. Just past the bridge on the right is the next conservation area of **Coldharbour. The Gun, No 44,** one of the oldest pubs along the river, provides sweeping views of Blackwall Reach. There are some 19th century houses built for the West India Dock Company along this road. Further along is the former **River Police Station, No 45, Nelson House, No 46**, and also **Isle House, No 47**. Lord Nelson is said to have stayed at Nelson House and Lady Hamilton used to go to the Gun Pub for her secret meetings with him. The Isle House was built in 1824 to the design of Sir John Rennie for the West India Dock Company's Blackwall Dockmaster.

Leaving Coldharbour and heading northward along Preston Road you find the early 19th century **Bridge House, No 48**, which was built to the design of John Rennie Senior for the Superintendent of the West India Dock Company. It has a fine Doric porch and Georgian elevation. A short distance further and you will find the **Brunswick Public House** facing the **Hydraulic Pumping Station, No 49**, built near the end of the last century to provide hydraulic power to operate cranes and lock gates in the nearby **Poplar Railway Dock, No 50**. Note the renovated 1960 crane and the old dock wall. Turn right at the roundabout and following the Docklands Light Railway elevated track you come to the second **Hydraulic Pumping Station, No 51**, at East India Dock Road. Built in 1857 this station provided hydraulic power for use in the former East India Docks and is now a Grade II Listed building. Overlooking the station is the new **East India Office Complex** and nearby is the **Financial Times** building. Walking further east past the big roundabout you see the remains of the **East India Dock Wall**, c1806. Across the bridge to the Royal Docks you will find to your right the confluence of the river with the Thames with a number of wildlife developments. The Limmo site is on the last loop of Bow Creek where the River Lee joins the Thames and adjacent to the old East India Dock Basin. The £3.5million scheme has created a park for visitors and children to enjoy and learn. Also on the river side is **Trinity Buoy Wharf and Lighthouse**, which was for 185 years the centre of Trinity House, the company responsible for the operation and maintenance of all lighthouses around the UK coastline. The beautiful octagonal lighthouse is unique and was built around 1860. Walk back from the crossing to the elevated DLR **Brunswick Wharf, No 52**, station and catch the train to the City or your next destination.

Billingsgate Market
LDDC, The Ledger Building
Canary Wharf
Heron Quays
Millwall Dock
Asda Superstore
Cannon Workshops
Video Theatre
Coach Tours
London Docklands Visitor Centre
RECEPTION
RESIDENTS CAR PARK
THE GUN
KILLICK
BOW CREEK ECOLOGY PARK - LIMMO
Willow coppice compartments
DLR viaduct
Small lake for pond d
Limmo Peninsula
East India Dock Basin
City of London
River Thames
Isle of Dogs
A11
A1205
A13
A1011
A102
A206

16
18
31
43
London Docklands
Interpretation centre and water intake from Bow Creek
meadow
Water filtration demonstration
Children's water activity area
Rainwater flood meadow
Car park
Docklands Light Railway embankment
New lagoon
into Bow Creek
ISLE OF DOGS
SOUTH QUAY
MILLWALL
CUBITT TOWN
ASPEN WAY
WESTFERRY ROAD
MANCHESTER ROAD
PRESTONS ROAD
MARSH WALL
A1206
River Thames
Westferry
Poplar
West India Quay
Canary Wharf
Heron Quays
South Quay
Crossharbour
Mudchute
Island Gardens
Blackwall
East India
Canary Wharf Pier
West India Pier
London Arena
Asda
Daily Telegraph (Works)
Mudchute City Farm
Millwall Park
Masthouse Terrace Pier
Greenwich Pier
Greenwich Maritime Museum
Newcastle Drawdock
1 - 8
9
10
11
12
13
14
15
16
17
18
19
20
21
22
23
24
25
26
27
28
29
30
31
32
33
34
35
36
37
38
39
40
41
42
43
44
45
46
47
48
49
50
51
52
KEY
Docklands Strategic Highways
Docklands Light Railway lines & stations
LDDC Offices
Jubilee Line (Under Construction)
East London Line
London City Airport
Fire Stations
Hospitals
Parking
Police Stations
Schools / Colleges

Southwark, Surrey, Wapping and Royal Walks

Southbank and Surrey Quays Walks
For many visitors to the area, Docklands will be a new experience. In the following pages a series of heritage trails and walks are given, describing historic landmarks and new developments. The first trail covers the South Bank, Bermondsey, Rotherhithe and Surrey Quays. It forms an interesting walk through the Southwark riverside and historic warehouses.

This riverside walk starts at **London Bridge, No 1,** which marks the upstream limit of the Pool of London. **Southwark Cathedral** on the west side of Borough High Street had its origins over a thousand years ago. Cross the road and make your way along Tooley Street past London Bridge Station to Hays Galleria which is part of the impressive **London Bridge City redevelopment, No 2**. This is a breathtaking conversion of Victorian warehouses into a superb shopping and leisure centre. Opposite is the **London Dungeon, No 3**, which exhibits a gruesome display. Moored along the river is the cruiser **HMS Belfast, No 4**, which was launched in March 1938 and retired as a floating barracks in 1963. She was moved to the Thames and opened to the public in 1971 as a museum. Further along is **St Olave,s School** which is a Grade II listed building.

Walk along Tooley Street to the south side of **Tower Bridge** where there is a hydraulic pumping station museum. Cross the road into Shad Thames. Along this road and facing the river are some of the finest Victorian warehouse conversions in Bermondsey. You pass the **Anchor Brewhouse, No 5**, which was a former Courage Brewery, once owned by the Thrale Family, friends of Dr Samuel Johnson, and the magnificently converted warehouses of **Butlers Wharf, No 6**. A great sense of drama is created by the high rise buildings on the bank of the Thames, enclosing the canyon with bridges called **Shad Thames** and other narrow streets. Further along is the **Design Museum, No 7**, displaying a selection of mass produced consumer goods from around the World with the **Bromah Tea and Coffee Museum** nearby. Just past Butlers Wharf is the historic and fascinating **St Saviours Dock, No 8,** and the area around Mill Street has a number of interesting 19th century buildings and also the splendid **Most Holy Trinity Church** of 1960. High warehouses include the charming Grade II listed **Christians Wharf** overlooking the dock. On the east side of the dock are **Vogan Mill** which is dominated with its new white tower soaring above the converted warehouses. The last group of warehouses are part of the **New Concordia Wharf, No 9**, and date from 1885. The nearby **Bermondsey Wall, No 10**, takes its name from the river embankment built for flood protection from the Thames.

A short distance down river from St Saviours Dock is **Cherry Garden Pier, No 11**, where you will find the **Angel Public House, No 12**, dating back to the 15th century when hospitality was offered by the Monks of Bermondsey Priory. **The archeological site, No 13**, closeby, contains the remains of King Edward III manor house Continue walking east and you arrive at **St Mary's Church, No 14**, in Rotherhithe close to the underground station. Built by local shipbuilders in 1715 on the remains of an older one of Saxon times. Opposite is the rectory, adjacent to which is a delightful little 18th century school house.

Overlooking the river is **Thames Tunnel Mills, No 15**, a fine example of early 19th century warehouse architecture. Adjacent to this building is the 17th century riverside ale house, the **Mayflower Public House, No 16**. In 1620 the sailing ship, Mayflower, moored here prior to her departure to Plymouth and her journey to America with the Pilgrim Fathers. The captain of the Mayflower, Christopher Jones, and many of his crew are buried in the nearby graveyard of St Marys, a church full of reminders that Rotherhithe was once a village of seafarers, shipbuilders and dockers. Nearby in Mary Church Street is the **Brunel Pump House Museum, No 17**, which was built by Marc Isambad Brunel to house the steam engines which drained the Thames tunnel. It was the world's first underwater thoroughfare. It is now a museum which tells the story of the tunnel and includes a restored steam engine. Visiting is by prior appointment. Close by Rotherhithe Street is the **London Glass Blowing Workshop, No 18**, where you can see glassblowers at work and buy their products.

Strolling along Rotherhithe Street eastwards you come to **Lavender Pond, No 19**, which used to be a shallow lake where timber from the Surrey Docks was floated for temporary storage. The pump house was built by the Port of London Authority in 1928 and the building now acts as a centre for a small nature reserve locally. There is a wildlife trail from Lavender Pond Nature Park south to **Russia Dock Woodland, No 20,** and Stave Hill Ecological Park at the centre of the Surrey Docks peninsular. **Stave Hill, No 21**, is an artificial hill 65ft. high which affords excellent views of Docklands and the City. At Stave Hill there is a brass scale model which shows how the area looked when the docks were operational.

From Stave Hill walk eastwards to **Surrey Docks Farm, No 22**, which provides a valuable education and community resource to local schools. Travelling south, you reach **Greenland Dock, No 23**, originally built in 1700 and redeveloped early 19th century. The entrance lock still has many of the original working features, such as the hydraulic capstans and rams. Use the restored footbridge and head for the **South Dock**. Enjoy the marina with its water- based leisure facilties. Then visit **Surrey Quays No 24**, shopping centre near the tube station. Near the exit you will find the late 19th century **Dockmasters Office, No 25**.

Heritage Trail in Wapping & Limehouse
Starting at the Tower of London you will notice the adjacent **Tower Bridge, No 26**, the western gateway to Docklands. It is of Victorian Gothic architectural design and a masterpiece of engineering opened in 1894. It has a central drawbridge, though it is rarely open these days. The high walkway affords magnificent views of London and the Thames.

On the north east side of the bridge is **Tower Thistle Hotel, No 27**, which provides 834 beds and conference facilities for 250. **St Katharines Docks, No 28**, is now established as one of London's most popular waterside attractions. The area provides a fascinating mix of old and new buildings housing offices, shops, restaurants, and pubs against a background of traditional boats and yachts which are moored in the dock. **Dickens Inn, No 29**, is at the heart of the complex. This former brewery warehouse has been converted into a pub and two restaurants. St Katharine Way leads to the **Hermitage Entrance, No 30**, of the former London Docks which was opened in 1820. Walk along the new canal to **Tobacco Dock, No 31**, the splendid Grade I Listed building built between 1810-1814 to store tobacco, but later used to keep precious furs and hence the nickname "Skin Floor". Across the Highway is the Church of **St George in the East, No 32**. From Tobacco Dock follow Wapping Lane to the High Street.

Wapping is a delightful area in which it is possible to recapture a sense of Dickensian London from the redevelopment of the area with conversions of historic buildings. Stroll along Wapping High Street and look at the elegant houses at **Wapping Pierhead, No 33**, built in 1814 for the senior officials of the London Dock Company. Adjacent to these houses is the **Town of Ramsgate, No 34,** which is a 17th century public house. Here, in 1688, the 'hanging' Judge Jeffreys was cornered by a lynchmob while trying to board a ship to Europe. He ended his days in the Tower of London. Alongside the pub is **Wapping Old Stairs**, one of the few remaining watermen's ferrying places along the river.

Just off the High Street in Scandrett Street is the site of Wapping's first church, **St Johns**, built in 1617 and has a small public garden. On the opposite side of the street is a tower which is all the remains of the second St Johns (1755-60). Further along Scandrett Street is **Wapping Sports Centre, No 35**, housed in a converted workshop where chains and ropes were made for the London Docks. There are public toilets on the corner of the street. Most of the former warehouses and buildings along the river frontage are Grade II Listed and have been beautifully renovated as luxury homes. These include Olivers Wharf, adjacent to the Town of Ramsgate pub, which was the first warehouse conversion into flats. The Gothic style building of 1870 was built for a merchant

George Oliver. For a hundred years it handled general cargo and tea. Nos. **78-80 Wapping High Street, No 36**, are typical red brick wharves originally built in 1830 and now used as offices. Human bones were discovered during refurbishment in the 1980s which were believed to be the remains of a murder victim.

Further along the High Street is **Wapping Police Station, No 37**, which dates from 1910 but it is on a site of the 1798 headquarters of the first UK Police Force. The small museum documents the aspects of the history of Docklands and the River Thames. Past the Police Station is **St John's Wharf, No 38**. A warehouse conversion formerly used for the storage of coffee, dried fruit and gum. The ground and first floors of the small adjoining warehouse are occupied by a public house **"Captain Kidd"**, which is close to the Old **Execution Dock** where Captain Kidd and other pirates of the 17th century came to a dead end.

Just downstream is **King Henry's Wharf, No 39**, a group of warehouses formerly owned by Alexander Tugg Company. Further along are the residential conversions of **Gun Wharves, No 40**, adjacent to Wapping Station. Built during the second half of the 19th century, the wharves were used for the handling of tea, canned goods, caskwork and general cargo. The High Street leads to Wapping Wall and past the converted warehouses is the **Prospect of Whitby, No 41**. Further along is **Shadwell Basin, No 42**, seven acres of water which used to have the largest inner city water centre in Britain. Captain James Cook was a parishioner of **St Paul's Church, No 43**, overlooking the basin and his eldest son was christened there in 1763. The Church has strong nautical associations with 75 sea captains buried in the churchyard. On the south side of the basin you will see the **London Hydraulic Pumping Station, No 44**. Built in the 1880s it was in operation as the World's last public hydraulic pumping station until its closure in 1977. It provided hydraulic power for machinery in the docks. At **King Edward Memorial Park, No 45**, you can have fine views of the Isle of Dogs and Rotherhithe.

From Garnet Street, cross Glamis Road Bridge onto The Highway and follow the road east, the large riverside development is on the site of **Free Trade Wharf, No 46**, which was one of the busiest private wharves in London. Two of the original saltpetre warehouses have been renovated. Further along the Highway you come to **Narrow Street** where you can explore the Regents Canal Dock now called **Limehouse Basin, No 47**, and also the canal tow path. Along Narrow Street is the **Grapes Pub, No 48**, which is said to have been used by Charles Dickens as the model for "Six Jolly Fellowship Porters" in his novel "Our Mutual Friend". To the east is **Limekiln Dock, No 49**, an old pottery site dating back to the 17th century. A few minutes walk northwards brings you to **St. Anne's churchyard, No 50** with its peaceful gardens. From Limehouse Station you can visit the Royals, take the DLR to Beckton.

Exploring The Royal Docks

The Royal Docks were once the greatest dock complex in the world, and currently largely undeveloped. Anglers and water sports enthusiasts avail themselves of the large tracts of water, while at Beckton skiers enjoy themselves on England's largest dry ski slope.The **Connaught Tavern, No 51**, near the DLR Royal Albert station, is an attractive building which was a public house used extensively by dockers until 1980. It was designed by Vigers and Wagstaffe in 1881 and is listed Grade II and so is the cast-iron urinal outside it. The architects also designed the **Central Buffet, No 52**, and **Gallions Hotel, No 53**, all of which have been renovated. Cross the Connaught Bridge and follow the road south to North Woolwich Road and **St Marks Church, c1862, No 54,** becomes visible. This former church has been converted into the Museum of Victorian Life. Walking westward, at Silvertown the main feature is the **Tate & Lyle Warehouse Building, No 55**. High on the north west faÁade of the 1930s Portland stone building is the famous golden syrup symbol of the lion and the bees, chosen by Abraham Lyle in 1883. In the tidal basin road near the **Windsurfing Centre, No 56**, on the Royal Victoria Docks, you will find the water **Pumping Station** designed by Richard Rogers to look like a ship. There are a number of parks as well as the **Newham City Farm** where you will find rare domestic breeds and farmyard animals.

29
CHARRINGTON
41
47
THE GRAPES
48
DICKENS
46
FREE TRADE WHARF
28
LONDON CITY AIRPORT
50
31
Bank
Fenchurch Street
CITY OF LONDON
Swan Lane Pier
A3 LONDON BRIDGE
Tower of London
Tower Stairs
London Bridge City Pier
H.M.S. Belfast
Hay's Galleria
Southwark Crown Court
London Bridge
TOOLEY STREET
London Bridge City Park
26
27
28
30
33
34
51
52
LOWER LEA CROSSING
SILVERTOWN WAY
VICTORIA DOCK ROAD
A1010
Custom House
Royal Victoria
East India
East India Dock Basin
Orchard Place
Blackwall Pier
Jetty
Reuters Jetty
Thames Wharf
Western Gateway
Gate 5
56
Royal Victoria Dock
West Silvertown Urban Village
Spine Road
Evelyn Road
North Woolwich Road
London City Airport Pier
55
Knights Road
Bradfield Road
Lyle Park
Manhattan Wharf
North Greenwich
Gate 2
Pontoon
River

Shadwell
LIMEHOUSE LINK
LIMEHOUSE BASIN
THE HIGHWAY
A1203
King Edward VII Memorial Park
Shadwell Dock Stairs
Ratcliffe Cross Stairs
Duke Shore Stairs
WAPPING
News International
SMITHFIELD
PENNINGTON
ST. KATHARINE DOCKS
Marble Quay
St Katharine Pier
ST KATHARINE'S WAY
Alderman Stairs
HERMITAGE BASIN
Wapping Sport Centre
Wapping Gardens
Wapping Health Centre
Wapping
Wapping Dock Stairs
King Henry's Stairs
Wapping Pier
Wapping Old Stairs
Wapping New Stairs
Wapping Police Pier
New Crane Stairs
Pelican Stairs
Globe Stairs
Pageant Stairs
ROTHERHITHE STREET
SALTER ROAD
B205
Rotherhithe Pier
Hanover Stairs
Church Stairs
Prince's Stairs
King's Stairs
Rotherhithe
BRUNEL ROAD
ROTHERHITHE
Ecological Park
Stave Hill
Russia Dock Woodland
DOWNTOWN
SURREY WATER
CANADA WATER
Canada Water
SURREY QUAYS
REDRIFF ROAD
BRUNSWICK QUAY
GREENLAND DOCK
SOUTH DOCK MARINA
Greenland Pier
Dog & Duck Stairs
St. George's Stairs
LOWER ROAD
A200
Surrey Quays
Butlers Wharf Pier
Horselydown New Stairs
Jacob's Island Pier
BERMONDSEY WALL WEST
BERMONDSEY WALL EAST
Cherry Garden Pier
Cherry Garden Stairs
Fountain Stairs
JAMAICA ROAD
BERMONDSEY
Bermondsey
SOUTHWARK LB
River Thames
Strategic Highways
Railway lines & stations
(Under Construction)
Airport
1km
½ mile
1000yds
50 48 49 47 45 46 32 43 42 31 44 41 28 29 27 30 35 40 39 36 38 33 34 37 19 6 7 9 10 8 11 12 13 14 15 16 17 18 20 21 22 23 24 25
36 37 38
CYPRUS
New Beckton Park
South Beckton District Park
PENNYROYAL AVENUE
ARMADA WAY
DOCKS ROAD
Gallions Reach
Connaught Roundabout
Royal Albert Roundabout
STRAIT ROAD
Visitors' Centre Open April 1995
Royal Albert
ROYAL ALBERT WAY
Beckton Park
Beckton Park Roundabout
Cypress Roundabout
Cyprus
Pumping Station
Gallions Roundabout
Proposed Royals Thamesmead Bridge
ROYAL ROAD
LEYES ROAD
CONNAUGHT ROAD
51 52 53 54
ROYAL DOCKS
ROYAL ALBERT DOCK
ALBERT BASIN
LONDON CITY AIRPORT
Runway
Terminal
KING GEORGE V DOCK
WOOLWICH MANOR WAY
Newham Community College
Gallion's Yacht Lock Entrance
King George V Flood Barrier and Lock
King George V Dock Entrance
Airport Roundabout
HARTMANN ROAD
CONNAUGHT ROAD
NORTH WOOLWICH ROAD
North Woolwich Roundabout
NEWLAND STREET
ALBERT ROAD
A1011
NORTH WOOLWICH
WOODMAN STREET
A117
Silvertown for London City Airport
SILVERTOWN
North Woolwich
PIER ROAD
Royal Victoria Gardens
Waldair Wharf
North Woolwich Pier
Woolwich Ferry Pier
Tate & Lyle Jetty
Thames
4
5

Tower of London and St Katharine Haven

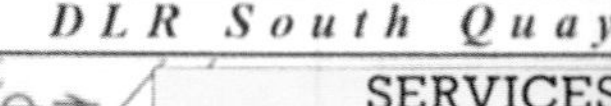

DLR South Quay

Docklands

WHERE TO GO

1 **Tower of London**: historic palace, prison and treasure house, with dungeons and the spectacular Crown Jewels.
2 **Tower Bridge**: the high-level walkway provides extensive views over London and the river Thames.
3 **St. Katherine's Dock**: historic shipping moored beside the old warehouses; shops and restaurants.
4 **Whitechapel Art Gallery**: exhibitions by artists of international repute; bookshop, cafe. (Not Saturdays).
5 **Petticoat Lane Market**: several streets of stalls, especially clothing; Sundays only.
6 **St. George's in the East**: early eighteenth-century church by Hawksmoor, pupil of the famous architect of St. Paul's Cathedral, Sir Christopher Wren.
7 **Tobacco Dock**: last remaining section of the former London Docks, about to become a stylish shopping centre
8 **Prospect of Whitby**: sixteenth-century pub with riverside seating and good food.
9 **Shadwell Park**: pleasant gardens and walks with views over the river Thames.
10 **St. Anne's Limehouse**: another Hawksmoor church; interesting tombstones in churchyard.
11 **Pennyfields**: famous throughout London for the Chinese restaurants in West India Dock Road.
12 **Stratford Market**: covered shopping centre with excellent food stalls, especially Fridays and Saturdays.
13 **West India Docks**: London's first enclosed wet docks (1802) with original warehouses and historic ships.
14 **Business Efficiency Centre**: services for Docklands businesses; restaurant.
15 **Mudchute Park**: green open space, horse riding, small farm, pleasant walks and views.
16 **Island Gardens**: riverside park with dramatic views across the water to Greenwich. DLR Information Centre open 11.00-16.00, in Station.
17 **Greenwich**: craft and antique markets, maritime museum, famous sailing ships Cutty Sark and Gipsy Moth.
(Travelling weekends and evenings? Check the railway is running.)

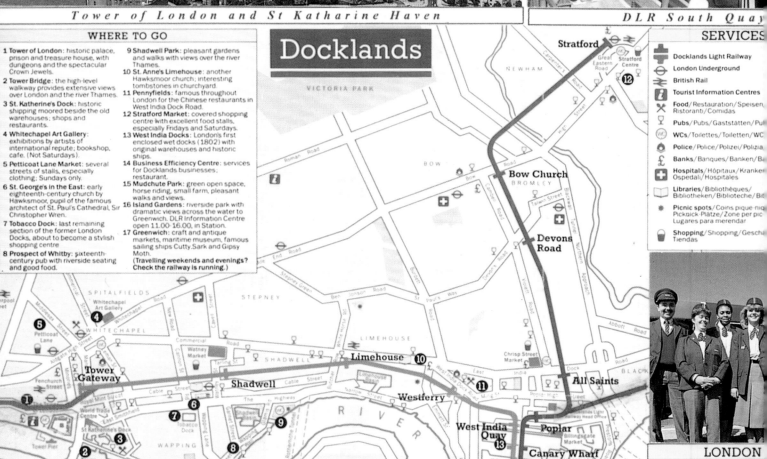

SERVICES

- Docklands Light Railway
- London Underground
- British Rail
- Tourist Information Centres
- Food/Restauration/Speisen/Ristoranti/Comidas
- Pubs/Pubs/Gaststätten/Pu
- WCs/Toilettes/Toiletten/WC
- Police/Police/Polizei/Polizia
- Banks/Banques/Banken/B
- Hospitals/Hôpitaux/Kranke Ospedali/Hospitales
- Libraries/Bibliothèques/Bibliotheken/Biblioteche/Bi
- Picnic spots/Coins pique-niq Picknick-Plätze/Zone per pic Lugares para merendar
- Shopping/Shopping/Gesch Tiendas

Stratford · Bow Church · Devons Road · All Saints · Poplar · West India Quay · Canary Wharf (opening late) · Heron Quays · South Quay · Crossharbour · Mudchute · Island Gardens · Westferry · Limehouse · Shadwell · Tower Gateway

LONDON

At all other times service will operate normally.
Further weekend and evening closures will follow after October.
Because of the nature of the work involved these dates may change but we will keep you well informed at all times.
For up to date travel information please phone 01-222 1234.

on, Isle of Dogs

LIEUX A VISITER

ower of London: palais historique et
rison renfermant des trésors, avec
es dongeons et les fameux Joyaux
e la Couronne.
ower Bridge: la passerelle
upérieure offre une vue panora-
ique de Londres et de la Tamise.
t Katherine's Dock: navires
istoriques ancrés près des ancients
ntrepôts, boutiques et restaurants.
hitechapel Gallery: expositions
ar des artistes de réputation
nternationale, librairie, café (fermé
e samedi).
etticoat Lane Market: étalages
épartis sur plusieurs rues, offrant
urtout des vêtements. Ouvert le
dimanche soulement.
t George's in the East: église du
ébut du 18ème siècle par
awksmoor, élève de l'architecte
enommé de la cathédrale St Paul,
ir Christopher Wren.
obacco Dock: la dernière partie qui
ubsiste des anciens Docks de
ondres, qui sera bientôt
ransformée en un centre
ommercial d'un style différent.
ouverture vers la 17 fin de 1988).
rospect of Whitby: pub du 16ème
iècle avec terrasse sur la Tamise, qui
ropose une cuisine appétissante.

9 **Shadwell Park**: jardines et promenades agréables avec vue sur la Tamise.
10 **St. Anne's Limehouse**: une autre église de Hawksmoor, avec des tombes intéressantes dans son petit cimetière.
11 **Pennyfields**: coin renommé pour ses restaurants chinois dans West India Dock Road.
12 **Stratford Market**: un centre commercial couvert avec un excellent choix de nourriture, surtout le vendredi et le samedi.
13 **West India Docks**: les premiers Docks protégés de Londres (1802) avec des entrepôts d'origine et navires historiques.
14 **Business Efficiency Centre**: une gamme de services pour les affaires au sein de Docklands, ainsi qu'un restaurant.
15 **Mudchute Park**: espace vert avec centre d'équitation, une petite ferme, des promenades et un paysage agréable.
16 **Island Gardens**: parc en bordure de la rivière offrant un beau panorama englobant la Tamise et Greenwich. Bureau de renseignements ouvert de 11h à 16h en gare.
17 **Greenwich**: avec boutiques d'antiquaires et d'artisanat, le musée de la Marine et les fameux voiliers Cutty Sark et Gipsy Moth.
(Pour tous déplacements le soir ou le weekend, s'assurer qu'il y a des trains.)

NFORMATIONSBROSCHÜRE FÜR TOURISTEN

ower of London: Historischer
alast, Kerker und Schatzkammer
mit Verliesen und den berühmten
Kronjuwelen;
ower Bridge: Der Hochweg über die
rücke bietet ein ausgiebiges Pano-
ama über London und die Themse;
St. Katherine's Dock: Historischer
afen mit neben den alten
agerhäusern vertäuten Schiffen;
eschäfte und Restaurants;
Whitechapel Art Gallery: Werke von
ünstlern internationalen Rangs;
Buchladen, Café (Samstag
geschlossen);
etticoat Lane Market: Mehrere
Straßen mit Ständen vor allem für
extilien; nur Sonntag geöffnet);
St. George's in the East: Von
Hawksmoor, Schüler des berühmten
rchitekten der St. Paul's Cathedral
Christopher Wren, im frühen 18.
ahrhundert erbaute Kirche;
Tobacco Dock: Der letzte
verbliebene Abschnitt der alten
Londoner Dock-und Hafenanlagen,
der nun in ein elegantes
Einkaufszentrum umgewandelt
werden soll; (Eröffnung im Herbst
1988).
Prospect of Whitby: Ein "Pub" aus
dem 16. Jahrhundert am Wasser mit
gutem Essen;

9 **Shadwell Park**: Hübsche Gartenanlage mit Spazierwegen und Aussicht auf die Themse;
10 **St. Anne's Limehouse**: Eine weitere Kirche von Hawksmoor mit interessanten Grabsteinen auf dem Friedhof;
11 **Pennyfields**: In ganz London berühmt für die chinesischen Restaurants in der West India Dock Road;
12 **Stratford Market**: Überdachtes Einkaufszentrum mit ausgezeichneten Imbißständen, vor allem am Freitag und Samstag;
13 **West India Docks**: Londons erster, 1802 gebauter Binnenhafen mit den ursprünglichen Lagerhäusern und historischen Schiffen;
14 **Business Efficiency Centre**: Dienstleistungen für das Hafengewerbe mit Restaurantbetrieb;
15 **Mudchute Park**: Weitläufige Parkanlage mit Reitschulen, einem kleinen Bauernhof, angenehmen Spazierwegen und Aussichten;
16 **Island Gardens**: Parklandschaft am Wasser mit eindrucksvoller Aussicht über den Fluß nach Greenwich; DLR Informationszentrum geöffnet von 11.00-16.00 uhr im Bahnhof.
17 **Greenwich**: Straßenmärktefur Kunstgewerbe und Antiquitäten, Schiffahrtsmuseum und die berühmten Segelschiffe Cutty Sark und Gipsy Moth.
(Fur Fahrten am Wochenende und den Abendstuden vergewissern sie sich bitte, ob die Strecke in Betrieb ist).

LUGARES PARA VISITAR

Tower of London: palacio, prisión y casa de tesoros históricos, con sus mazmorras y las espectaculares Joyas de la Corona.
Tower Bridge: el viaducto de gran altura ofrece extensas vistas panorámicas de Londres y el río Támesis.
St. Katherine's Dock (Muelle de Sta. Catalina): barcos antiguos anclados junto a los viejos depósitos; tiendas y restaurantes.
Whitechapel Art Gallery: exposiciones de artistas de fama internacional; librería y cantina (cerrada los sábados).
Petticoat Lane Market: varias calles de puestos de venta, especialmente de ropa.
St. George's in the East: iglesia de principios del siglo XVIII diseñada por Hawksmoor, discípulo del famoso arquitecto de la Catedral de San Pablo, Sir Christopher Wren.
Tobacco Dock (Muelle del Tabaco): último sector en existencia de los famosos Muelles de Londres, a punto de convertirse en elegante c-ntro comercial. (se inaugura en el ontóno de 1988).
Prospect of Whitby: pub del siglo XVI con asientos frente al río y buena comida.

9 **Shadwell Park**: acogedores jardines y paseos con vistas del río Támesis.
10 **St. Anne's Limehouse**: otra iglesia de Hawksmoor; interesantes tumbas en los jardines circundantes.
11 **Pennyfields**: famoso en todo Londres por los restaurantes chinos de West India Dock Road.
12 **Stratford Market** Mercado de Stratford): centro comercial techado con excelentes puestos de comida, especialmente los viernes y sábados.
13 **West India Docks** (Muelles de West India): los primeros muelles húmedos techados de Londres (1802), con depósitos originales y embarcaciones históricas.
14 **Business Efficiency Centre** (Centro de Eficiencia Comercial): servicios para las empresas de la zona de Docklands; restaurante.
15 **Mudchute Park**: espacio verde abierto, equitación, pequeña granja, agradables paseos y vistas.
16 **Island Gardens** (Jardines Island): parque a la margen del río con espectaculares vistas por sobre las aguas hasta Greenwich. DLR Centro de Información Abierto de 11.00 a 16.00 en la estación.
17 **Greenwich**: mercados de artesanía y antigüedades, museo marino, los famosos veleros Cutty Sark y Gipsy Moth.
(¿ Va a viajar en fines de semana o por las noches? Verifique que el tren esté funcionado.)

DOCKLANDS RAILWAY HERITAGE TRAIL

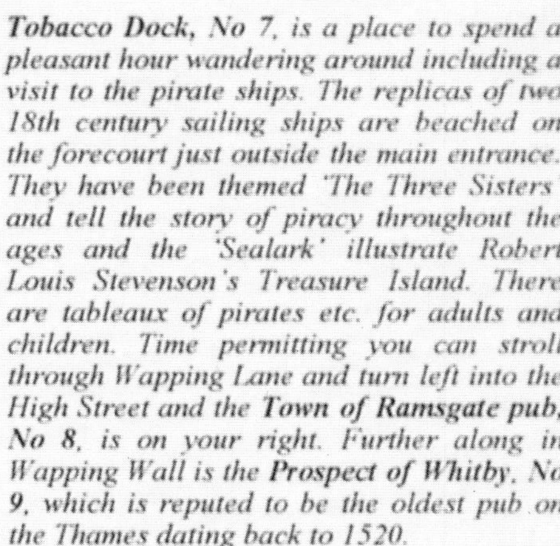

London's historic Docklands is one of the most fascinating areas of London, a place to absorb both the Londoner and the visitor. It is an area of huge and vivid contrast, a place where a new city for the 21st century has been created in an old city boasting a proud and colourful past stretching back to Roman times. A quick glance at the map here will reveal just some of the many places of interest. The areas around each DLR station offer the visitor many attractions. There are many walks which can be enjoyed together with specialist restaurants, pleasant parks and gardens, and urban farms. Apart from the dockland areas the visitor can wander further north into the historic districts of East London. On this side you will find a guide for a day's outing, the trail starts from Tower Hill and ends at Island Gardens. Enjoy your visit and walk.

The Circle tube line takes you to Tower Hill station. From the station side of the street you can get a splendid view of the ***Tower of London, No 1****. You can then cross the road to have a closer look and wander around the outside of the Tower, eventually making your way along the embankment and under* ***Tower Bridge, No 2****, to* ***St Katharine's Docks, No 3****. Built by Thomas Telford in 1828 and closed for shipping in 1968, it was the first of London's dockland areas to be developed in the early 70s. This area is a lovely place to stroll with plenty to see including the fibreglass elephants guarding the East Smithfield entrance. In the background there is a sound of water splashing gently against the quay side. The World Trade Centre houses the London Commodity Exchange and also offers a range of services to business people including conferences and other administrative facilities.*

Walk northwards through Leman Street to Aldgate and Whitechapel areas. ***The Whitechapel Art Gallery, No 4****, was founded early in the 20th century and its aim is to bring art and culture into the lives of east-enders. The gallery which has been extended specialises in exhibitions of the avant garde. One of the oldest markets in London is* ***Petticoat Lane market, No 5,*** *which is of 17th century origin, when sellers of old clothes established themselves here. The market has been quite popular over the past two centuries and is still extremely busy at weekends with its stalls of clothes etc. Brick Lane is where bricks and tiles were manufactured in nearby fields and brought into London along this route in the 16th century. It is now the area of east London where Bengali communities live, they have a number of restaurants.*

You can take a bus from Tower Hill to Tobacco Dock or DLR to Shadwell Station. ***The Church of St George in the East, No 6****, is an English Baroque architectural masterpiece dating from the 18th century.*

Tobacco Dock, No 7*, is a place to spend a pleasant hour wandering around including a visit to the pirate ships. The replicas of two 18th century sailing ships are beached on the forecourt just outside the main entrance. They have been themed 'The Three Sisters' and tell the story of piracy throughout the ages and the 'Sealark' illustrate Robert Louis Stevenson's Treasure Island. There are tableaux of pirates etc. for adults and children. Time permitting you can stroll through Wapping Lane and turn left into the High Street and the* ***Town of Ramsgate pub, No 8****, is on your right. Further along in Wapping Wall is the* ***Prospect of Whitby, No 9****, which is reputed to be the oldest pub on the Thames dating back to 1520.*

Pick up the Docklands Light Railway at Shadwell, the trains are computer controlled and driverless - they stop automatically if there is an obstruction on the line. An excellent feature of the railway is that you spend the entire journey at a high level and get splendid views of the historic part of London's docks. You can proceed to any station along the line and visit ***St Anne's Church, No 10****, and* ***Pennyfields, No 11****, at Limehouse,* ***Stratford Market, No 12****, further north, or alight at* ***Canary Wharf, No 13****, and the nearby conservation area. Near Crossharbour Station is the* ***Docklands Visitor Centre, No 14****, (previously the Business Efficiency Centre). You can also alight at Mudchute Station and make your way onto the* ***Mudchute, No 15****, commonly known as the 'muddy' which is a 32 acre park near Asda Superstore. There is riding, school, allotments, wetland called the 'New Tye' where local children study newts, frogs and other aquatics, and Mudchute Urban Farm. There are cattle, pigs, ducks, chickens and other animals ideal for children seeing these creatures for the first time.*

You can make your way to ***Island Gardens, No 16****, and gaze across the Thames at the Royal College, one of London's most famous riverside buildings. Down through the foot tunnel under the Thames and up to Greenwich with the famous* ***Cutty Sark, No 17****. There are arts and crafts, restaurants and cafes, pubs with beer gardens around the area then walk onto the* ***Royal Maritime Museum,*** *Royal Observatory and snaps for the album standing on the famous Meridian Line. You can go back to the pier to take one of the special* ***Thames Barrier*** *boat trips to see the eighth wonder of the world. Returning to Greenwich pier, you take the return journey back to* ***Westminster or Tower Pier*** *by riverboat. It is also a good way to see the riverside rejuvenation of Docklands all the way back to Charring Cross or Westminster Piers.*

HERITAGE TRAIL IN GREENWICH

Greenwich is rich in heritage and full of interest and entertainment. Here you will find the National Maritime Musuem, the Royal College and the Cutty Sark. It has a range of craft shops as well as the Greenwich Market which is open at weekends. Greenwich Pier is an ideal place to start and end your visit. You may also cross the river by the foot tunnel at Island Gardens station. The walk through the tunnel takes about 6-10 minutes. Greenwich British Rail station is also convenient for travel from Waterloo. Along the river front is TheTea Clipper, The ***Cutty Sark, No 1****, which was built in 1869 and made the fastest voyage for a sailing ship between Australia and England in 1887. Nearby is the* ***Gypsy Moth IV, No 2****, which came to Greenwich in 1968 after being sailed single-handed around the World in 226 by Sir Francis Chichester. Walk south and on your left are the finest group of historic buildings in the area, the* ***Royal Naval College, No 3****, which were developed by Wren in 1692. Once this was a palace for the Tudor Sovereigns and the birthplace of King Henry VIII. During the 18th century it was adapted as the Greenwich Hospital for Naval ratings. Inside see the magnificent painted hall by Thornhall where the body of Lord Nelson lay in state in 1805 before the procession along the river to St Pauls Cathedral. Cross Romney Road and you are in the Greenwich Park and opposite is the* ***Great National Maritime Museum, No 4****, which has the finest maritime collection in the World. An extensive range of model ships, naval weapons, uniforms and paintings are exhibited. See how life has changed at sea during the past 500 years, since the days of Drake, Raleigh and Nelson. To the east side is the* ***Queen's House, No 5****. Built by Inigo Jones this beautiful house was completed for the Queen of Denmark in 1619. The spectacular circular tulip staircase is similar to the one designed by Palladio in Venice. Walking uphill through Greenwich Park you come to the* ***Old Royal Observatory****, No 6, the home of Greenwich Mean Time where you can stand astride the Greenwich Meridian. Designed by Christopher Wren it was built for King Charles II in 1658. On the west side of the Observatory is* ***Flamstedd House****, No 7, which was the residence of the Astronomer Royal until 1948. The octogon room designed by Wren has been restored as it would have been in the 17th and 18th centuries with contemporary clocks and telescopes. Find your way through the park to the Greenwich Village Centre and along the High Road is the impressive St Alfege Church which is a 17th century masterpiece by Hawksmooor and is dedicated to St Alfege.*

Following their raid on Canterbury in 1012, the Danes brought St Alfege to Greenwich and murdered him on the site where the church stands. Follow the river front eastwards past the Royal Naval College to Trafalgar Tavern. Built in 1830s it was a place where writers gathered including Charles Dickens. It was once famous for its whitebait suppers. Members of Parliament would charter boats to come here and enjoy themselves after a sitting. Walk back to the pier and catch a riverbus to Tower or Westminster Pier.

SPECIAL EVE

Greenwich is always full of life. Inside the museums, in the Park or by the Pier, you may come across costumed actors or musicians to add extra enjoyment to your visit. Use our recorded information line for details of special events.

You can't imagine a finer ceilling.

OLD ROY

Stand astride
See the Time-
simulations a
timekeepers a
Flamsteed stu
stairs to the b
maybe fit in a

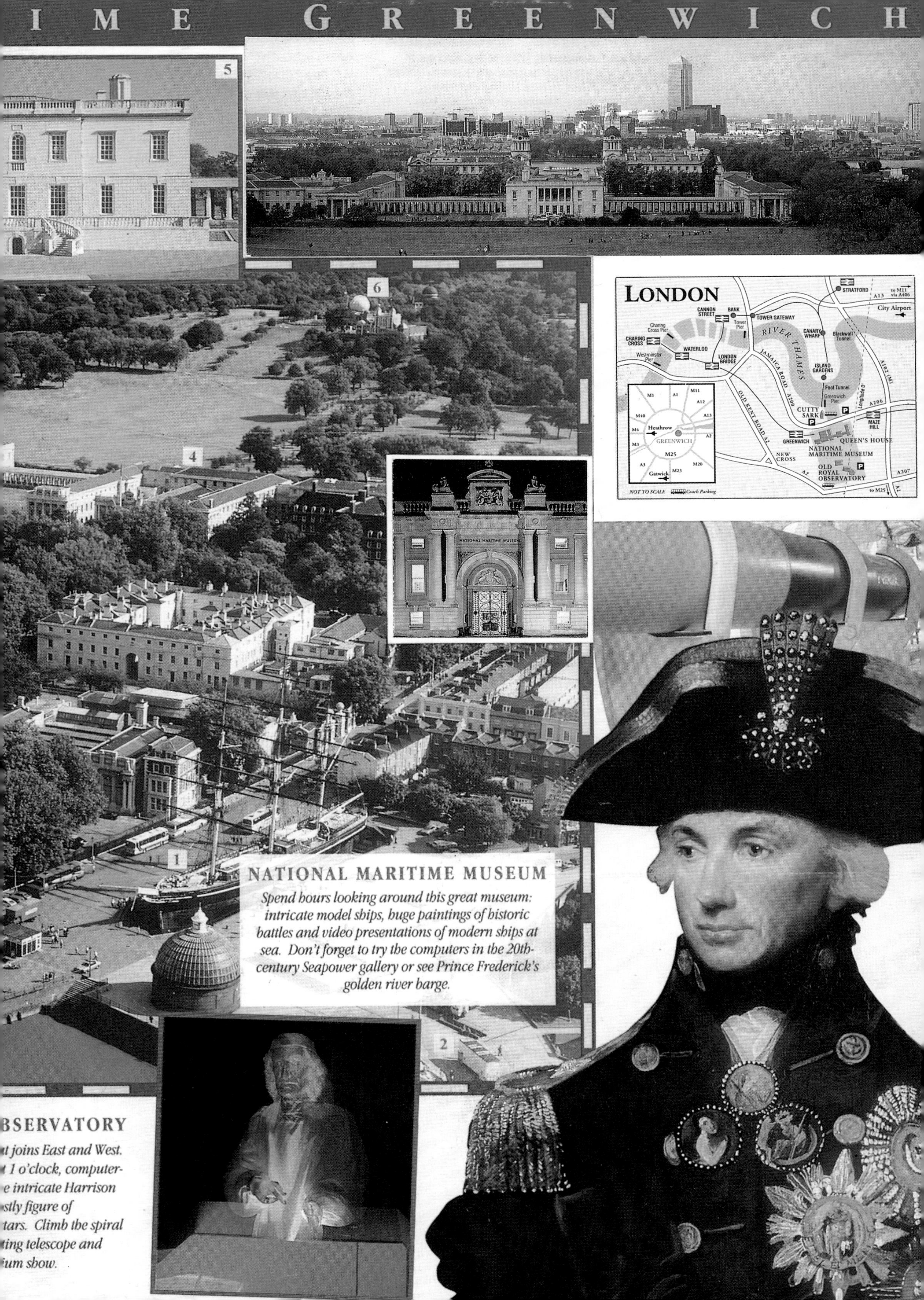
IME GREENWICH
5
6
4
1
2
LONDON
CANNON STREET
BANK
TOWER GATEWAY
STRATFORD
to M11 via A406
A13
City Airport
Charing Cross Pier
CHARING CROSS
Tower Pier
RIVER THAMES
CANARY WHARF
Blackwall Tunnel
Westminster Pier
WATERLOO
LONDON BRIDGE
JAMAICA ROAD A200
ISLAND GARDENS
A102 (M)
Foot Tunnel
Greenwich Pier
Longitude 0°
M1
A1
M11
A12
M40
Heathrow
A13
M4
GREENWICH
A2
M3
M25
A3
Gatwick
M23
M20
OLD KENT ROAD A2
CUTTY SARK
A206
MAZE HILL
GREENWICH
QUEEN'S HOUSE
NATIONAL MARITIME MUSEUM
NEW CROSS
OLD ROYAL OBSERVATORY
A2
A207
NOT TO SCALE
Coach Parking
to M25
NATIONAL MARITIME MUSEUM
NATIONAL MARITIME MUSEUM
Spend hours looking around this great museum: intricate model ships, huge paintings of historic battles and video presentations of modern ships at sea. Don't forget to try the computers in the 20th-century Seapower gallery or see Prince Frederick's golden river barge.
BSERVATORY
t joins East and West.
t 1 o'clock, computer-
e intricate Harrison
stly figure of
tars. Climb the spiral
ting telescope and
ium show.

Globorama plans back on track
Revised design and development plans for London's proposed Globorama electronic observatory tower, conceived as a landmark for the national millennium celebrations, were unveiled this week by G Maunsell & Partners, the consulting engineer and initiator of the project. The 200m-high tower will be sited on the Meridian at Victoria Deep Water Terminal on the Greenwich peninsular, adjacent to the Millennium Exhibition site.
CABOT PLACE WEST
BANK OF ENGLAND
DORSET ARMS
WHITBREAD
PIER TAVERN
CHARRINGTON
The Telegraph
THE WATERFRONT
E BRUNSWICK A
THE GUN
GOOD FOOD SERVED AT THE BAR
CHARRINGTON
LORD NELSON
THE GEORGE
THE QUEEN
HE CUBITT AR
Taylor Walker
WATERMANS ARMS

Britain's Millennium Exhibition 2000

Millennium Commission and Exhibition

The Millennium Exhibition will provide the time and the place for the UK to show the World what Britain can achieve. It will embrace the whole nation in a shared vision, bringing together the successes of the past and aspirations of the future, to provide hope and inspiration for the nation as we enter the next Millennium.

The Millennium Commission considered four potential sites for the exhibition but in March 1996, chose a site on the Greenwich Peninsular to host the year long fair in the year 2000. The site owned by British Gas, facing Canary Wharf, offered the greatest potential and met the Commissions aspirations. It is believed that it could attract more visitors and allow more exciting presentation of the exhibition theme, as the site is on the Prime Meridian Line and the Imagination proposals for Greenwich feature the circle of time. The Millennium Exhibition will regenerate an important part of southeast London and breathe new life into a wasteland close to the heart of the Capital. British Gas has started decontamination and preparation work on the heavily polluted area. Such a potentially permanent entertainment and leisure development, together with residential and retail space would create new economic opportunities for the area and stimulate further regeneration of the remaining British Gas holdings on the peninsular.

Top left: (a) Cabot Square and Cabot Place at the centre of Canary Wharf. Right: (b) Maps of Royal Docks, including London City Airport, Canary Wharf and Greenwich Peninsular, where the Millennium Exhibition will be held. (c) The proposed 600ft (183m) high Globorama Tower for the Greenwich Peninsular. (d) South Bank proposed Ferris Wheel. Five times higher than the Big Wheel at Blackpool, the Millennium Wheel is a giant 500ft (152.5m) diameter Ferris Wheel which could be sited on the River Embankment. The Wheel, which would be capable of carrying over 2000 people per hour around its circumference, has already aroused controversy. (e) Snapshots at Canary Wharf. Middle (f)The East End of London is celebrated for its pub culture. On the Isle of Dogs there was a pub on almost every corner before the Blitz. Most pubs were built when the Isle was industrialised during the 19th century. The working day for dockers, shipbuilders and factory workers was long and dirty, and the pub was a place for a thirst-quenching pint. Others, such as the Waterfront was the first pub of the new era. Bottom: (g) Aerial view of the Isle of Dogs looking south. (h) View of historic maritime Greenwich showing the Royal Naval College and the Greenwich Peninsular.

Millennium Awards and Organisation

The Commission received over two hundred responses to the consultation proposals on the Millennium Awards. There were many imaginative and exciting suggestions from training social entrepreneurs, to oral history project, to exchanges of experiences across the UK. The majority of responses stressed the importance of community initiatives, and the role the awards might play in strengthening communities by releasing the talent and energies of individuals to a wider benefit. The importance of the award offering opportunities to people from all sections of society; young and old; all ethnic and faith groups; all levels of ability; were also strongly endorsed. The first headline theme for the award became "You and Your Community".

The programme organisation will see the development of a series of regional centres to shape the context of the exhibition itself. In year 2000 each region will have a week in the exhibition programme to deliver their vision of the new century. Artistic, scientific, historical and sporting components from the regions will be incorporated into the exhibition.

The Millennium Commission has made public its financial commitment for the exhibition with a pledge of up to £200million from lottery grant; the remaining capital and operating costs to be raised from other sources.

Greenwich Millennium Trust

The Greenwich Millennium Trust was set up to represent local London interests and ensure that the exhibition provides a sustainable legacy for the local people. The Greenwich Borough Council was represented on this Trust. More than sixty groups in all were represented on the Millennium Trust Forum. The Millennium Commission was determined that the Exhibition would be visionary, a time of romance, entertainment and excitement for the people of Britain. Its legacy could be nothing less than the transformation of London for future generations. It is hoped that all these ambitions come together neatly at Greenwich and mark a contribution to the nation.

Operation by Imagination Limited

London based design company, Imagination Limited, chosen by the Millennium Commission as the operator for this national exhibition to conceive ideas, designs, finances, develop and operate the exhibition. The Company took the theme of time as a central part of the exhibition, and revealed their plans for twelve themed pavilions, with a "central circle" each focusing on a different interpretation of time. In historic Greenwich, home of the Meridian Line from which the World measures Greenwich Mean Time, past, present and future would be linked in this event of a lifetime.

Ferris Wheel at South Bank

This giant structure has been proposed and sponsored by British Airways to mark the Millennium. On board one of the 16-seat cabins you would be whisked skywards where from the top a great view of London is promised, and should the weather be right, views far west of Windsor and as far east as Rochester in Kent. The wheel will dominate the skyline along the South bank of the Thames. At £5.00 per adult and £2.50 for children, passengers will be carried in 16 enclosed carriages for a ride lasting up to 20 minutes. The wheel, 152m diameter, is expected to cost around £10million to build with British Airways looking to the money markets for private sector finance.

At 500ft (152.5m), it promises to be the fourth highest structure in London. For comparison, the Canary Wharf Tower is 800ft high and Big Ben just over 300ft. More than half the energy to keep the wheel rotating at a steady one foot per second will come from the River Thames. In high winds it may sway about a little but it is very unlikely that anyone will feel nauseous or sea-sick. The plan is to operate it by the Thames for five years before moving it to a permanent location in another part of the country. The final decision on whether to build it rests with the Planning Department at Lambeth Council.

Globorama Tower

Plans to build a 600ft. (183m) high tower on the Greenwich peninsular have also been presented which would offer unparalleled views of London. The Globorama tower would dominate the site of the Millennium exhibition with six observation decks using the latest computer and satellite technology to link visitors to different parts of the globe. Other attractions could include theme rides, conference facilities, bars and restaurants. The concept is that they could build a tower not only that people could look out over London from but also at other levels they could actually look out at views in other cities around the world, perhaps other environmental sites, in real time. If the plans are agreed, the tower will be nearly as tall as the Canary Wharf tower. It is also on the line of the Greenwich meridian that runs from the Royal Observatory. There are similar observation towers in many other world cities. Globorama is half the size of the CN Tower in Toronto and only slightly smaller than the Eiffel Tower in Paris.

The Globorama project is expected to cost £90 million to build and its backers are hoping for a substantial grant from the Millennium Commission to help pay for it. Greenwich Council is in the process of deciding whether to grant them planning permission.

London Docklands into the 21st Century
The Royals - Jewel in Docklands Crown

Assessment of Regeneration

The London Docklands Development Corporation (LDDC), was set up under the Local Government Planning & Land Act of 1980. The size of the urban development area is 8½ sq.miles covering 5,500 acres (2,226 hectares). At the end of a decade of economic regeneration i.e. 31 March 1991, an estimated £8.5 billion was committed by the private sector in the area. The cummulative Government grant receivable for this period was almost £1.2 billion. This generated an estimated private to public investment ratio of 7.5 : 1. Located in the Isle of Dogs Enterprise Zone, Canary Wharf is the flagship of the regeneration programme, and its tower is the most visible building on the London skyline. It arouses many feelings and has been the subject of much media attention and discussion. The development when fully built will be the World's largest office building, consisting of about 12million sq.ft of office and commercial space.

The Enterprise Zone

In 1982 the Enterprise Zone was created in the former West India Docks complex. For a period of ten years it offered commercial developments with exemption from rates, development land tax on site disposal up to 1985, relaxation of planning controls, exemption from training levies and the need to provide Government statistic, and 100 percent tax allowance for building construction cost which included the cost of site preparation, landscaping and access roads. Another important element of the capital allowances was the fact that they could be claimed for an indefinite period after the expiry of the Enterprise Zone in April 1992 provided a building contract had been signed before the expiry date. The scheme was of considerable success in attracting private investment.

Funding

As a Government Agency the Corporation had no shareholders and was not intended to make a profit. It spent all its money on achieving the regeneration of the Dockland area. It had two sources of income, the first being Government grants, part of an overall amount agreed by Parliament for urban regeneration throughout Britain. The second source of income was from the sale of land for development. In the early 80s disused dock lands plus some other areas in public ownership were acquired. After clearing the land and putting in roads and drainage, the sites were sold or leased. The increased attraction of Docklands resulted in a major rise in land values. Land values for housing schemes away from the more expensive waterside rose from less than £100,000 per acre in 1982 to between £500,000-800,000 per acre in 1988. Success was derived in this strategy by spending approximately £1.6 billion in attracting over £11 billion of private investment by 1998. The investment has come from Britain and abroad from businesses, banks and pension funds.

Employment and Population

Most people living in Docklands either worked in the docks or related industries and during the decade or so after the closure of the docks 18,000 dock related jobs were lost with unemployment reaching 24% by 1981. Local industries continued to decline through the early 1980s and it wasn't until 1986-87 before new companies started to arrive. There has also been a welcome move of newspapers into Docklands. In addition a significant number of jobs have been created in tourism including hotels and catering. Since 1981 when there were 27,000 jobs in Docklands, by 1996 there were nearly 65,000.

Community Response & Impact

On the downside, the Corporation did not fare as well as it would have liked in bringing along the local councils and communities, many of them with understandably strong points of view. The relationship with Tower Hamlets, Southwark and Newham Councils was for many years inevitably combative. With the increase in construction momentum and revenues post 1987, attitudes significantly improved. The Corporation was keen to encourage and assist initiatives by local people.

Housing

The overall strategy aimed to widen housing choice in terms of size, style, price and tenure, and also to improve the quality of existing housing stock as an essential process to attracting and retaining residents and to bring about social and economic regeneration. The main aim was to promote the growth of home-ownership and secure some affordable housing. The demand for expensive homes was met by privately developed schemes and privately owned land. Cumulative figures up to 1991 showed over 15,000 housing units completed and another 1600 to be built giving a total of 16600. It was forecast that a further 20,000 units could be built on the remaining site.

Handing over of Docklands

During 1995 it was announced that the LDDC would be handing back Docklands to the local authorities formally in March 1998 and negotiations started between the two sides. Beckton was handed back to Newham Borough Council in January 1996. Local Authorities are determined to adopt a pro-active role in the economic regeneration of the area.

Prospects of Canary Wharf

In 1802 the West India Docks opened with a flourish. They were the glittering centrepiece of civil engineering works. In January 1992 a fine group of buildings which make up the first phase of Canary Wharf in London Docklands were completed. Although separated by 190 years, both were pinnacles of their age. During 1993, the collapse in demand for office space from city firms was soon made worse by the general recession in the south east. Transport problems made the area even harder to sell as a business location. Ultimately this led to the liquidation of the Company. By 1995 the trend had reversed and more companies moved into the Tower. The Jubilee Line construction has created an upward trend to make Canary Wharf the focus of attention. One day when the dust has settled and time is available for reflection, Canary Wharf will be recognised as one of the great adventures in design and construction. It stands as a tribute to all those involved - a monument to endeavour which should stand long enough to celebrate its bicentennial, a feat already achieved by The London Docks.

Future Development of Docklands

It is difficult to estimate just how much impetus has been created in the years of the regeneration. Despite a stormy ride it has created an economic sub-culture where things continued to happen into the 1990s. The regeneration can be measured in real terms, but there is a lot more to be done. On the Isle of Dogs the focal point is the massive Canary Wharf development. Only half the available wharf has been built on so far. Behind the tower, coffer dams for deep foundation work are ready, but on hold. Here, another two towers and other blocks would double the size of the project. (See inside back cover).

To the east the huge Royal Docks, as yet undeveloped, present a jewel in Docklands regeneration. For both the business community and for local people the new opportunities offered are certain to grow as we go into the 21st century. Previous developments elsewhere were criticised for lack of infrastructure being put in place before development began. This accusation cannot be levelled at the Royal Docks. While developers chewed over their plans, road schemes and the DLR extension to Beckton have pushed ahead. The vital bridge across the River Lea opened in 1991, ahead of schedule. The Limehouse link in 1993 completed the excellent connection to the city. The Jubilee line extension has given much needed mass-transit access to the area, supplementing the light railway. A third tunnel at Blackwall is planned, in addition to the proposed East London river crossing, connecting the North Circular and Royal Docks to highways south of the Thames.

There have been a number of proposals for development over the years but only few have materialised and the opportunities therefore are tremendous. Wimpey has already commenced

The Shape of things to come? Top: (a) and (b) A new shopping and leisure development, including the Museum of Docklands, called Port East on the North Quay of the Isle of Dogs. Middle: (c) A life of variety and quality at Canary Wharf. (d) Model of a new footbridge spanning the Royal Victoria Dock. Bottom: (e) Transforming the Royal Docks into The Water City of the 21st Century. (f) London's Canary Wharf when completed. (g) The Financial Centre in New York, USA.

the building of 1500 new homes for the urban village on the south quay of the Royal Victoria Dock. An exhibition centre has secured Government support for the proposal under a Private Finance Initiative. Another project of great importance is the Royals University College, catering for 5000 students on a 25 acre campus on the north side of the Albert Dock. Courses, planned by the University of East London, cover Architecture, Technology, Business & Management, Art, Design & Fashion, and Media Communications.

London World Financial Centre

London is ideally positioned with a foot in each of its rivals, namely Tokyo and New York, working days. But the City, despite the recent planning relxation, is high on know-how but low on land resources. In the City office occupation costs are relatively high and the standard of floor-trading is limited. This fact will get more firms looking towards less expensive areas and more modern trading floors such as at Canary Wharf. The International financial service organisations feel that to compete in the global financial markets they must be in London alongside their competitors. They regard London as the premier financial centre and there are nearly 500 foreign banks represented in London more than in New York and Tokyo. The big prize is the title World Financial Centre and the fortune that goes with it. London currently holds the prize but New York is right up there on its tail. Docklands has boosted London's chances over the past decade and will continue to do so into the 21st century.

Exploring Museums in and around Docklands

Explore Ships and Museums
The Maritime theme is represented by three ships, which can all be boarded and viewed: **HMS Belfast, No 16,** the World War II cruiser, by Hays Galleria near Tower Bridge, the Katherine and May, **No 19** , a 3-masted top-sail schooner, near Southwark Cathedral and London Bridge, and the **Cutty Sark, No 1**, the famous tea clipper at Greenwich. Nearby is the **National Maritime Museum, No 2**, with its detailed historical account of Britain's naval history. Further south in Greenwich Park is the old **Royal Observatory, No 3**, where historical navigational instruments are on display. Military history is on view at Woolwich in two small museums, the **Royal Artillery Regimental Museum, No 4**. Further along the river on the south side you come to the **Thames Barrier Visitor Centre, No 5**, with a dramatic display of London "flooding" and the advanced technology which has gone into the flood barrier. Just across the river, a Victorian railway station has been converted into the **North Woolwich Railway Museum, No 6.**

When Marc Brunel built the first tunnel under the Thames at Rotherhithe, c1843, the civil engineering profession was in its infancy. The new exhibition at **Brunel's Engine House, No 7**, at Rotherhithe, tells the story of the eighteen year long construction process and the many lives lost. Also in Rotherhithe is the **Lavender Pond Pump House, No 8**, where some of the Docklands memorabilia collected from the Thames foreshore may be viewed. Further upstream at Butlers Wharf, the **Design Museum, No 13**, has exhibitions of mass produced goods from around the world. There are other attractions north and south of the Thames. These include the **Bethnal Green Museum of Childhood, No 11**, and the **Ragged School Museum, No 12**, illustrating the lives of East End families in the 19th century. An outstanding collection of photographs illustrating the social life on the Isle of Dogs from 1880s to the 1980s are kept by the **Island History Trust, No 10. The Museum of Docklands, No 9,** based on the North Quay of the Isle of Dogs, has a unique archive and exhibits relating to life and work in Docklands. Finally **Tower Bridge, No 14**, the world renowned lifting bridge, contains exhibitions describing its function, history and operation.

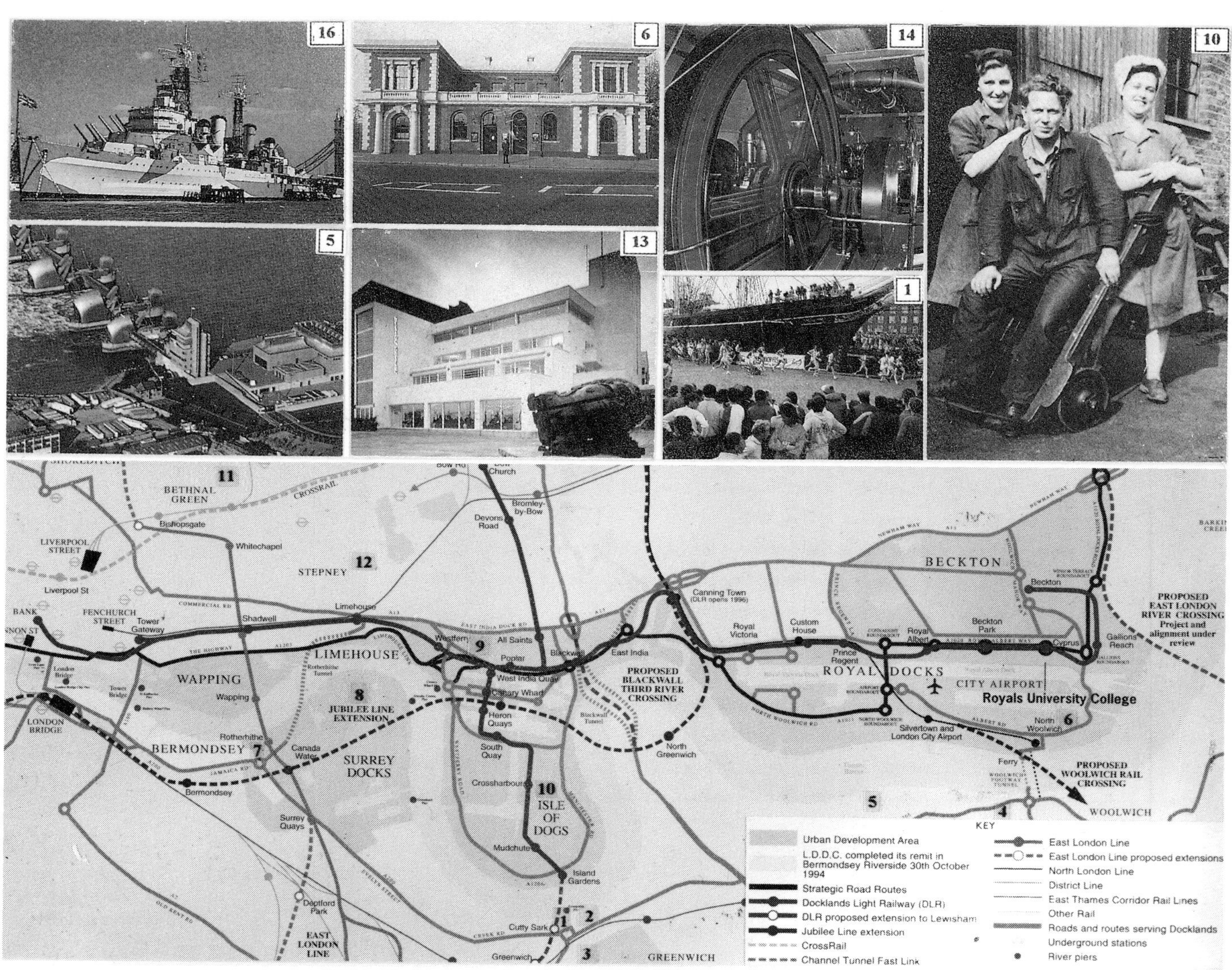

Map of London Docklands today showing the locations of the museums

Southwark Walk to Globe Theatre

Southwark, on the south side of the Thames, was a bustling maritime community from Roman times. The southwark riverside walk has some of the finest views of the City and St Paul's Cathedral just across the river. Passing Tower Bridge and following the river you will arrive at **Hays Galleria, No 15,** which was previously Hays Dock built by Cubitt in 1856 around the river Neckinger which flowed into the Thames. Take a few minutes detour to the old **Operating Theatre Museum, No 17**, at St Thomas' Street. This small museum is packed with a collection of historical medical instruments and a 19th century operating theatre where surgeons practised their skills on unfortunate patients! Back on the riverside path the walk continues beneath the arch of London Bridge into a paved area beside **Southwark Cathedral, No 18.**. This Cathedral dating back to the 13th century, has rich architectural features from Medieval to Victorian times. Shakespeare's brother Edmund is buried here. Walk on from the Cathedral to **Clink Street**, a narrow lane where can be seen a **Medieval Rose Window**, the remains of the Palace of the Bishop of Winchester, and its name is synonymous with prisons everywhere. It is said that the worldly Bishop once ran the Clink Prison on this site. The cruel way the prison was run and the life there is portrayed by the **Clink Prison Museum, No 20**, which has a gruesome collection of torturers tools.

Past Clink Street is **Bankside** where Londoners from the Middle Ages to the Civil War took a walk on the wild side with its theatres, boar and bear baiting pits, brothels and taverns. The most spectacular reminder of this district is the construction of the **New Globe Theatre, No 21**, in which the thatched wooden structure where Shakespeare's plays were performed has been recreated near to the presumed site of the original. The site of the 17th Century **Rose Theatre** where **Shakespeare** acted and Christopher Marlowe's plays were first performed, is nearby. Despite the uncovering of its foundations in 1989, the remains of the Rose are still hidden behind glass in the basement of an office block on the corner of Rose Alley and Park Street. In nearby Bear Gardens, the Shakespeare Theatre Musuem traces the development of the theatre in London from 1576 to 1642 underlying the history of Southwark as an important theatre home.

Bankside is being developed into a new cultural and social centre for London. The **Bankside Power Station, No 22**, is being converted into the new Tate Gallery to house the modern collection of Matisse, Giacometti, Henry Moore and others. This huge brick structure is an industrial giant echoing the shape of St Paul's facing it across the Thames. You can sit down on a bench overlooking the river and admire the views across the City and the riverside. This area is going to be changed over the next few years. It is worth visiting now in case the historic sites disappear for ever.

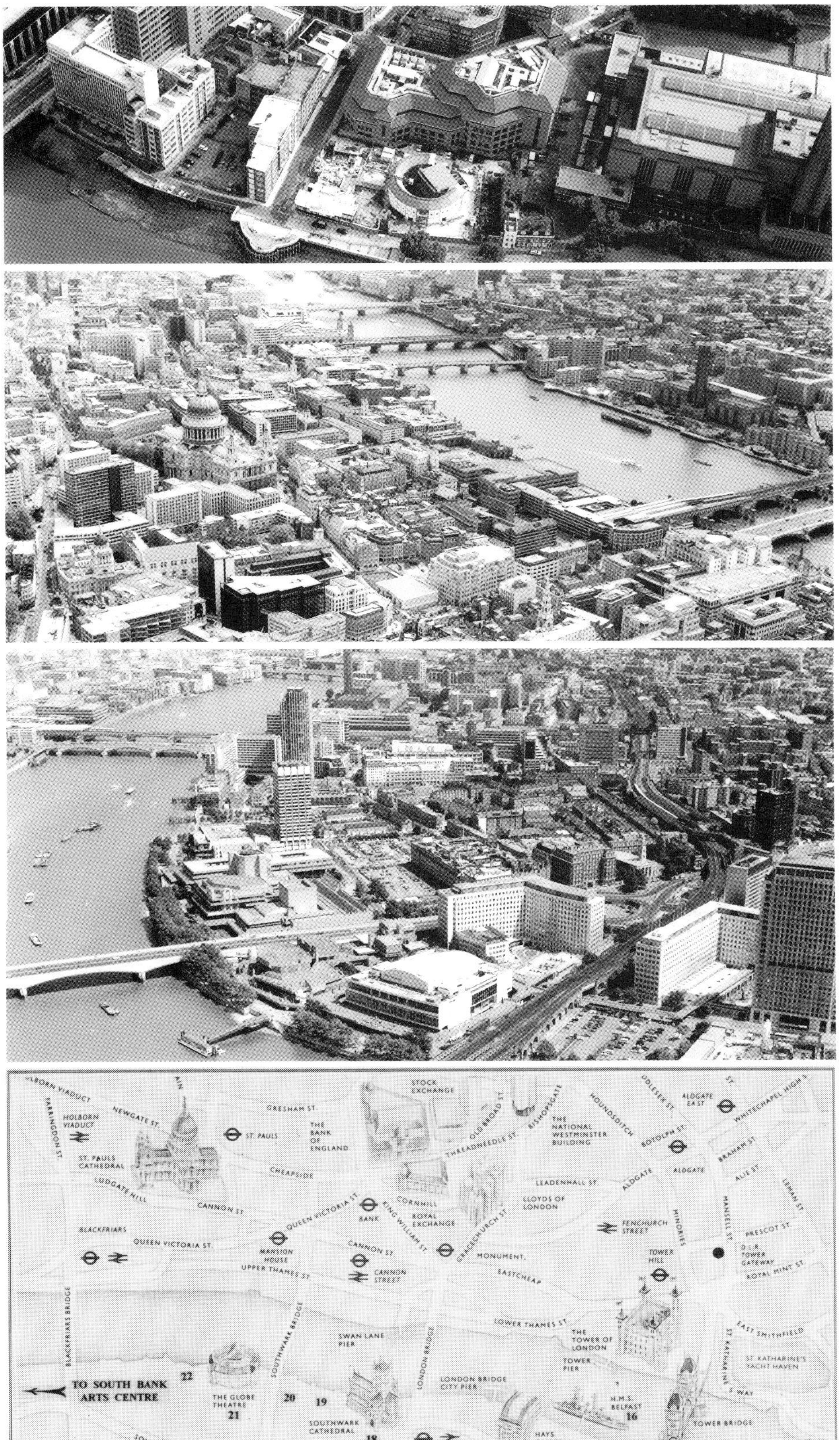

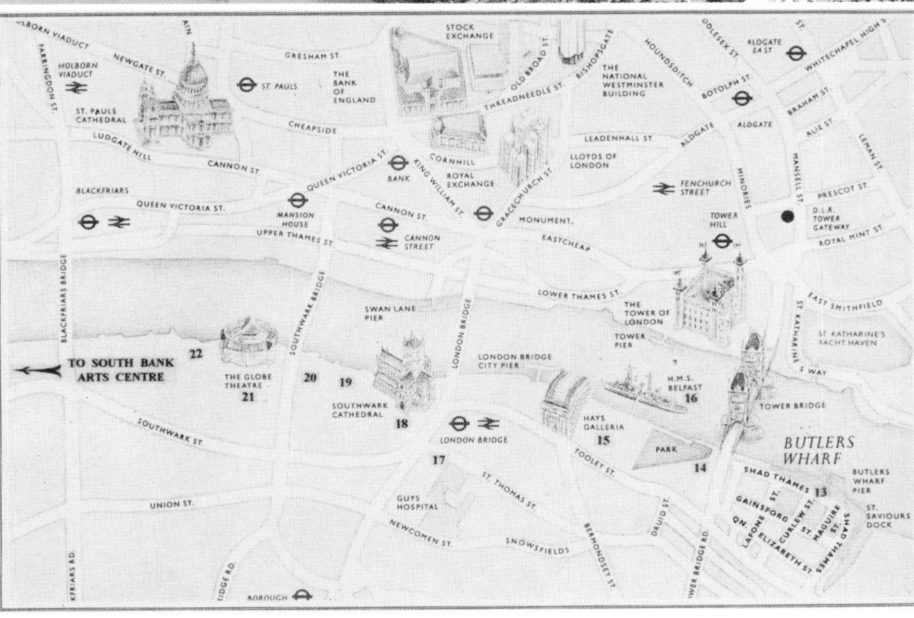

The Thames riverside from Tower Bridge to Waterloo Bridge, (a) The new Shakespeare Globe Theatre and Bankside Power Station. (b) View of the City and Southwark looking east, showing London Bridge City, Southark Cathedral and Globe Theatre. (c) The South Bank Arts Centre. (d) Map of Southwark and the City.

Dates from the History of London Docklands

43 Romans invaded Britain and crossed to London
61 Tacitus wrote of London as a Commercial Centre
70 Romans built the first wooden London Bridge
408 Romans withdrew from Britain
527 London became the Capital of the East Saxons
604 Venerable Bede recorded London as a seaport of many nations.
883 King Alfred captured London from the Danes and constructed Ethelredshithe on the Thames.
900 Wine merchants from Rouen settled at Dowgate.
1066 William the Conqueror granted a Charter to London
1275 First customs duty levied by Crown.
1382 First Customs House at Woolwich (Controller was Geoffrey Chaucer)
1515 Henry VIII sets up Royal Dockyards at Deptford and Woolwich.
1558 Elizabeth I established the Legal Quays along the City Waterfront.
1560 East India Company founded, with docks at Blackwall. Granted a Charter by Queen Elizabeth I in 1600.
1612 First Shipwright's Company established.
1700 Howland Dock was built in Southwark - name changed to Greenland Dock in 1763 and Commercial Dock in 1806.
1790 Brunswick Dock, Blackwall, opened.
1793 William Vaughan produced the first plans for the Wet Docks.
1796 A House of Commons Committee was appointed to plan docks for the increased trade and shipping.
1799 Parliament passed an Act to build docks on the Isle of Dogs.
1802 West India Docks opened.
1805 London Docks opened. City Canal opened.
1806 East India Docks opened (1,300 homes demolished to build it.)
1807 Surrey Docks opened.
1828 St Katharine's Dock opened (1,033 homes demolished to build it).
1850 Major Irish immigration into Docklands.
1855 Royal Victoria Dock opened.
1868 Millwall Dock opened.
1870 South West India Dock constructed.
1872 London dock strike for increased pay - successful.
1880 Royal Albert Dock opened.
1880-90 Major Jewish immigration into the East End
1886 Tilbury Dock opened.
1889 Great Dock Strike in London for 6d per hour - successful. Formation of first dockers' union.
1909 Nationalisation of unprofitable dock companies form Port of London Authority.
1920 London dockers strike for pay increase - successful.
1921 King George V Dock opened - funded by Government's unemployment programme.
1922 Formation of TGWU out of dockers' and other unions.
1926 London dockers joined General Strike.
1940 Mass bombings of Docklands began during the Second World War - including Black Saturday, 7 September, 430 dead, 1600 seriously injured, 10,000 homeless.
1943-4 Floating harbour built for D-Day landings
1954 London Dockers strike against compulsory overtime - unsuccessful.
1967 East India Dock closed.
1968 London Dock closed. Dock labour de-casualised.
1969 St Katherine's Dock closed.
1969-70 Major Asian immigration into the East End.
1970 Surrey Docks closed. First official London dock strike since 1926.
1972 London joined National Dock Strike.
1976 Docklands Joint Committee published London Docklands Strategic Plan.
1980 West India and Millwall Docks closed.
1981 Royal Victoria & Albert, and King George V Docks closed. LDDC began operations
1982 Enterprise Zone created on the Isle of Dogs.
1986 News International moved from Fleet Street to Wapping, becoming focus for disturbances
1987 Docklands Light Railway opened. London City Airport opened. Daily Telegraph and Guardian moved from Fleet Street to Isle of Dogs.
1988 Construction of Canary Wharf started on the Isle of Dogs. Dramatic regeneration.
1992 Canary Wharf Tower opened and tenants moved in.
1993 Olympia & York went into liquidation
1994 Daily Mirror moved from Holborn into the Tower.
1996 IRA bomb exploded damaging DLR station and buildings. Millennium Commission chose Greenwich for its exhibition.
1998 Opening of Jubilee Line Extension
2000 Britain's Millennium Exhibition on Greenwich Penninsular.

Top: (a) "The Idle Prentice turned away and went to sea" published by Hogarth in 1747, shows the windmills and gibbet on the Isle of Dogs. (b) Wyngaerde Panorama of London, c1543. (c) The Queen Mother in Surrey Quays 1988. Centre: The City sky line and old Canary Wharf 1984. Bottom: Cabot Square 1994, Butlers Wharf 1960 and 1994, and South Dock marina 1995.

Index

Illustrations not referred to in the main text have numbers shown in bold type.

William Shakespeare

Acknowledgements

I would like to express my gratitude to the University of East London for its support of the research work. I am very much indebted to numerous individuals, previous writers, photographers, estate agents and many diverse organisations who so kindly helped with the preparation of this book.

For the supply of considerable information and for the kind permission to reproduce photographs and illustrations, I am deeply grateful to the London Docklands Development Corporation (LDDC) and the Port of London Authority (PLA). I would tender my thanks to Mr Eric Sorensen, LDDC Chief Executive, and Ms Sunny Crouch, Director of Public Affairs. To Canary Wharf Development Company and Olympia & York special thanks are given for the support of the research work and the supply of many photographs, maps and illustrations.

For the generous supply of superb aerial photographs I am most grateful to Chorley and Handford, Safford Road, Wallington, Surrey. The assistance and co-operation of Tom Samson and Paul Proctor are most appreciated. Acknowledgement with many thanks has to be made of the large amount of information received from the Museum of London and the Museum of Docklands who have kindly supplied maps, photographs and slides. The dedication of the museum staff is commendable.

Much appreciation is due to the staff of the Guildhall Library and the Public Relations Department of the City of London Corporation for the supply of information and slides.

For assistance with the historical research I am deeply grateful to Terence O'Connell. Special thanks are due to Tom Juffs for his enthusiasm and unstinting support throughout the project. I would like to thank sincerely Linda Day for her help, excellent typing and patience in preparation of the whole manuscript with great care. I would like to express my thanks to Dr Kamel Hachouf in preparing the illustrations and to John Noble in compiling the index. I am most grateful to my wife, Irene, for her continued support and lasting patience.

For information on life and work in the docks, I am very grateful to many ex-dockers including Jack Dash, David Large, George Surridge, J Gibbs, Harry Read, George Exall , James Young and J C Wells.

Photographs were kindly supplied by various shipping lines including Ben Line, Ellerman Line, Harrison Line and Fred Olsen Line. Thanks are due to Captains G Nicholson , DJ Cranna and T Couchman, and to the artist Colin Verity.

Considerable information was supplied by many organisations including Docklands News, Docklands Magazine, Port of London Magazine, New Civil Engineer, Butlers Wharf Limited, St Martins Property Corporation, St Katharine by the Tower, Jacobs Island Company , Anchor Brewhouse, Barratt East London, Broseley Estate, Costain Homes, Daniel Homes, Ideal Homes, Heron Homes, Laing Homes, Lovell Farrow, Regalian Properties, Roger Malcolm, Waites Homes, Wimpey Homes, Rosehaugh co-partnership, Conran Roache, Tobacco Dock Development, Trafalgar House Residential, Wiggins Property Group, Colin Druce & Company, Docklands Light Railway, John Mowlem, Thames Line, the Daily Telegraph, Daily Mirror, the Independent and Times newspapers, Evans Tours, City of London Corporation, Greenwich Council and Tourist Board, Millennium Exhibition Trust, Millennium Commission, West Ham Library and its local history section, Thames Line, Imperial War Museum, Savilles Property, Bernard Marcus, Prudential Property, Carleton Smith, Healey & Baker, Clapshaws, Cluttons, Jones Lang Wooton, Grant & Partners, National Maritime Museum, National Rivers Authority, Trafalgar House.

I also thank many other people who helped including Lawrence Stratford, Joyce O''Neill, Angus Rankine, Kathleen Barnhill, Philip Plumb, Vivian Hamley, Mary Mills, Joanna Maddison, Geoff Nyberg, Gary Jewell, Terry Hatton, Roger Mutton, Grant Smith, Carole Anthony, Howard Bloch, Sheila Johnson, Ron McDougall, Paul Campfield, Peter Van Walwyk, Paul Smith, Sandra Zahra, Alan Hooker, Jenny Hall, Gavin Morgan, Ted Weedon and Ian Williams.

To members of the public who have kindly supported our publications, I express my deepest appreciation.

Inside of Back Cover opposite: Artist's impressions of the completed Canary Wharf complex in the 21st century.
Above: (a) Artist's impressions show possible future development on the Isle of Dogs and in the Royal Docks. (b) The SS Great Eastern which was designed and built by the innovative Victorian Engineer Isambard Kingdom Brunel. This famous ship was launched on the 31st January 1858 from Burrell's Wharf on the Isle of Dogs and was six times larger than anything afloat at the time and at 692ft (211m) long was over twice the length of the later SS Great Britain restored in 1980s at Bristol. Today, as in 1858, the Isle of Dogs is the centre of Britain's attention with the Enterprise Zone again helping create the giant Canary Wharf and providing opportunities and jobs for Londoners. Also one of the most well known landmarks along the river which has been standing for over 300 years is the Prospect of Whitby Public House in Wapping. Will the same thing be said about Canary Wharf in the 22nd Century?